Foreword by **Moody Black**

100 POEMS &
POSSIBILITIES
for HEALING

LAURA DI FRANCO

Stacy Belinsky, Richard Bredeson, DebS,
Thais Conte, Christine Falcon-Daigle, Nuria Gabitova,
Ashley C. Hall, Dawne Essence Horizons, Lisa Karasek, Guy Kilchrist,
Elizabeth Kipp, Yantra-ji, Heidi MacAlpine, David D McLeod,
Linda Aileen Miller, Ian Morris, Carole Park, Dr. Pamela J. Pine,
Silfath Sophia Pinto, Miko Reed, Zanzel (Moma Zey) Kathy Roach,
Dorri C. Scott, SkyyFlower, Jacqueline Solimini, Tanya Stokes,
Nydia Laysa Stone, Dinahsta "Miss Kiane" Thomas,
Lulu Trevena, Michol Tuttle, Emily Atlantis Wolf

Foreword by **Moody Black**

100 POEMS &
POSSIBILITIES
for HEALING

LAURA DI FRANCO

Stacy Belinsky, Richard Bredeson, DebS,
Thais Conte, Christine Falcon-Daigle, Nuria Gabitova,
Ashley C. Hall, Dawne Essence Horizons, Lisa Karasek, Guy Kilchrist,
Elizabeth Kipp, Yantra-ji, Heidi MacAlpine, David D McLeod,
Linda Aileen Miller, Ian Morris, Carole Park, Dr. Pamela J. Pine,
Silfath Sophia Pinto, Miko Reed, Zanzel (Moma Zey) Kathy Roach,
Dorri C. Scott, SkyyFlower, Jacqueline Solimini, Tanya Stokes,
Nydia Laysa Stone, Dinahsta "Miss Kiane" Thomas,
Lulu Trevena, Michol Tuttle, Atlantis Wolf

Get access to free writing and business resources
in the Brave Healer Resources Vault here:
https://lauradifranco.com/resources-vault/

DEDICATION

To Jude Christensen, who, with one simple sentence, "Thank you for sharing your poem with us," helped me know I was a poet.

To Ginny Robertson, who, with one simple request, "Can I use your poem in my magazine?" made me wonder what else was possible with my poetry.

To Laura Munson, who, with one simple statement, "I love poems that cut straight to the heart," validated my kind of poetry, and helped me give myself permission to write and share them.

And to Dinahsta "Miss Kiane" Thomas, who, with one simple invitation, "Would you like to be the featured poet at BusBoys on August 18th?" forced me to become the performance poet I thought I might could be.

And a note to all the friends of poets and lovers of poetry: keep encouraging your poet friends. One simple note may change their life.

FOREWORD
by MOODY BLACK

Healing. . .

. . . the word itself sounds like some stuff needs to be happening internally. I was ecstatic when I was asked to write a foreword to a book of poetry that is primarily based on healing. I say this because that word (healing) keeps popping up nowadays, almost to a point where it makes you wonder if it's time to start doing it. You know—heal. Then, you must ask yourself: *Why do I need to heal? What am I healing from?*

These poems reflect where we are with that (healing). A poetic wake-up call, if you will. As a matter of fact, Laura Di Franco challenges the reader to perform "Brave Healing." It sounds like the words don't belong together, but they do! There's a sense of bravery in taking the steps to heal. More importantly, understand that we can't change or improve the world if we don't start with ourselves. Laura emphasizes that in her introduction poem:

"What if we healed the wound

inside ourselves first?

That's the way we heal the world. . ."

Each stanza is a step-by-step guide to healing. Also, Laura's poem set the tone for the rest of the book. One of my favorite lines in the book comes from the poem *When the Sky Talks.*

"The sky would never

let me down.

She knows I only come

when my soul's at stake,

when I need to believe

in something more

sure"

Don't we all, at some point, look at the sky at our weakest and most vulnerable moments and question things, hoping the sky, in all its vast beauty and mystery, offers some kind of solace or resolution, especially when you are at your lowest point? To recognize and face that is an essential part of healing. To have what I like to call a "by yourself meeting." Those meetings can create something great out of the darkness, even if it takes several meetings!

This sentiment is covered in the poem *Reclamation:*

"I found myself at the bottom of a pit

so deep and dark

I didn't recognize me—again."

And these are just a few of the gems present in this beautiful book of endless possibilities—possibilities for healing! So, read—take the first step—heal.

Even through the harshest times, find the beauty. Thus, is the whole part of healing. Recognizing that at your lowest, there is an upside. You just have to be your motivational coach.

I have a poem about healing. Hopefully it'll help you with the journey:

Healing

By Moody Black

healing is self-love
a poem instead of a suicide note
at the same time, healing is a suicide note written by all the damaged parts of you
encouraging you to keep going
healing is knowing that you can't get rid of every damaged part of you
but you sure can put them in their place

healing is loving yourself with all those damaged parts of you
and sitting down with them in the room in the same place
healing is when you tell the person in the mirror, "i love you. . . and i can't change how the story started. . ."
but you look in your eyes and say. . .
 "it will not be how my story will end!"

TABLE OF CONTENTS

INTRODUCTION

Chapter 1 | 1

Open Mic Therapy: Healing at the Microphone

Laura Di Franco, MPT, Publisher

Chapter 2 | 16

Crack Open Your Soul with Poetic Vulnerability

Dinahsta "Miss Kiane" Thomas, MSW, Poet, Performer

Chapter 3 | 34

Metamorphosis

Thais Conte

Chapter 4 | 41

Unleash Your Healing Power!

Elizabeth R. Kipp

Chapter 5 | 52

Seeing Myself

Lisa Karasek

Chapter 6 | 61

Climb Coconut Trees to Cloud Mountains

Carole Park, Spiritual Chi Yoga Healer and Teacher

Chapter 7 | 69

Two Sisters: One Love - A Bond to Cherish

Dorri C. Scott, MSW, Exec MBA and
Zanzel (Moma Zey) Kathy Roach, MA

Chapter 8 | 92

Poetry as a Therapeutic Tool for Integration

Christine Falcon-Daigle, MFA, Global Sisterhood Circle Facilitator

Chapter 9 | 107

Honor Thyself, Heal Thyself

Guy Kilchrist

Chapter 10 | 115

Being Overwhelmed and Doing It Anyway

Stacy Belinsky

Chapter 11 | 124

Love Letter to My Missing Soul Sister

Emily Atlantis Wolf

Chapter 12 | 137

Nectar or Poison: Words Wound or Heal

By Lulu Trevena, Artist, Soulful Living Coach

Chapter 13 | 146

Ever Wish You Could Turn Back Time?

By Linda Aileen Miller, LMT, CD(DONA)

Chapter 14 | 155

Leaving Paris in Tears: Unlocking The Magic Within

Silfath Sophia Pinto, Wisdom Keeper, Somatic Artist, Spiritual Visionary

Chapter 15 | 168

The Heart Knows

Dr. Pamela J. Pine

Chapter 16 | 177

Out of a Black Hole into the Light

DebS, Energy Release Facilitator

Chapter 17 | 188

Burning Bright: A Poetic Journey of Self-Rediscovery

Nuria Gabitova, Edupreneur

Chapter 18 | 197

Seasons Change: All is Fair in Love and War

Tanya Stokes

Chapter 19 | 206

Align with Your Inner Truth

Ashley C. Hall, RYT-500

Chapter 20 | 214

A Healing Journey Through Community

Richard Bredeson

Chapter 21 | 225

Letting Love Lead – Living a Life of Freedom, Love, and Joy

Yantra-ji, Therapist, Artist, Author, Spiritual Teacher

Chapter 22 | 240

5 Ways to be Unstoppable After Divorce

Miko Reed

Chapter 23 | 250

From Unsure I'd Survive to Learning to Thrive

Michol Mae Tuttle, MSc

Chapter 24 | *262*

A Path Forward: Hatred's Antidote in Unity

Jacqueline Solimini, MPH

Chapter 25 | *269*

When Poetry Ignites Your Soul

SkyyFlower

Chapter 26 | *278*

Soul Sessions: Poetry as Therapy

David D McLeod, DD, PhD, Certified Master Life Coach

Chapter 27 | *292*

Awakening the Senses Through Grace and Community

Heidi MacAlpine, OTD, Educator

Chapter 28 | *301*

Whispers of Wisdom:
Secret Spells and Codes for Sovereign Survival

Nydia Laysa Stone, Somatic Healing Artist, Therapist, and Coach

Chapter 29 | 313

The Everything That No One Sees

Ian Morris

Chapter 30 | 327

Healing in the Pen: Writing for Wellness

Dawne 'Essence' Horizons, LMT, HHC

Chapter 31 | 335

The End is the Beginning of Everything Good

Laura Di Franco

INTRODUCTION

Laura Di Franco is my name, and brave healing is my game. . .
. . . and I thought we could do a little brave healing right now; sound
good?

Great, I'll show you how.

Rest your eyes.
Take a breath.
Feel the words
that are said.

Drop down inside.
Recognize
hiding isn't the answer.
Take a moment to feel everything.
Maybe you'll see
we all feel everything.

Nothing's really right or wrong.
It's all more like a song.
You like rock.
I like jazz.
But all music has a vibe
and it's the vibe we feel that's real.

No word or rhyme or melody
is better.
It all just depends on what jives
with your heart
what makes your soul light on fire
or dance
or sing
or express.

So maybe instead of killing each other
or dropping bombs
or trying to find something
the other did wrong
we could move to the sounds made of love.

What if we healed the wound
inside ourselves first?
That's the way we heal the world.

What if being born
automatically makes you worthy,
a living, breathing manifestation
of creative energy
with the power to heal.

It all starts with a feel.

You're a healer whether you know it or not.
Might as well be brave and start now.

What do you feel?

Can you feel yourself on this stage
out loud
with your message?
Or does the heat of unworthiness and shame
keep you afraid?

Fear's just a feeling
and it's stealing your show.
It's going to take
a brave kind of healing.

But I'm here today to tell you
anything's possible
when you wake up
fiercely alive
inside of your life
and decide
to make a change.

Brave healing.

It starts with a pause
and a breath
a check in
with your bod and your mind
knowing what feels good
and right to your soul.

Follow those sacred
breadcrumbs
until you're standing there
staring joy in the face
and both of you laugh
and say,
"Baby we've mastered this game!
Now it's time to play."

I remember learning poetry in school. After that experience, it's a small miracle you're reading this book.

I remember being graded on my memorization and recitation of a poem called Jabberwocky by Lewis Carroll. Unfortunately, what I remember is the pain of those moments, memorizing and then reciting in front of the class. I had such severe performance anxiety as a kid. Gosh, it was bad. I claimed the title of "severe introvert" and used that as a shield throughout most of my life.

I also remember being forced to analyze many poems in school. This felt like a waste of time. *If we're confused or don't know what they mean, then what's the point?*

Poems, to me, can speak easily to the soul. They don't need to be analyzed. They don't need to be a mystery.

If only they taught poetry back then the way I know it now—as a connection to my own soul, and a way to express it to the world, and as a way to heal—oh, how different things could've been.

It was after a fulfilling 30-year career in holistic healing when I took the stage again, claimed my voice, and stepped into my worth and power with poetry. Poetry did that for me! Over those decades, I wrote so many poems, many of which will never be read by anyone but me.

But it was the day I stood up in the middle of 220 people in a ballroom of healers in Sedona and recited a poem I wrote (the day before) when I received and claimed my title of "Poet." One of the people this book is dedicated to is Jude, the woman who helped me experience that life-changing moment. You can read that whole story in a chapter in our book, *On Purpose Woman*, by Ginny Robertson, another woman I dedicate *this* book to, who helped me claim my poet title by asking if she could publish one of my poems in her magazine.

I went on after the experience in Sedona to self-publish five books of poetry and begin sharing them out loud on open mic stages. It was moments on the stage in front of my poetry family where I continued to find my voice and practiced using it. It was those moments on stage, sharing my poems, that helped me dive a layer deeper into the unworthiness wounds and understand what I was here to do—what I was born for. Those moments were therapy for me.

I remember one of the first nights at BusBoys and Poets, a local venue here in the Washington D.C. area. I met my poet friend KaNikki Jakarta in Alexandria, Virginia. She is another friend who helped me earn and claim my poet title. I stood on the stage with my little crumpled-up piece of paper shaking so hard I knew the back of the room could see. And I spoke my poem despite the fear. Standing on that stage was healing. I'll tell you more of that story in Chapter 1.

For now, please get ready to bask in what's to come here—life-changing moments, stories, and transformational, healing poetry from thirty fellow poets whose desire it is to help you understand what's possible when you connect with your heart and soul—and poetry.

Whether you read it, write it, speak it, or are only just beginning to dabble in it, there are so many gifts here for you. Each chapter includes the poet's story, their poems, a writing prompt for you to enjoy, and their bio so you can get to know them better.

Ladies and gentlemen, next up to the microphone are my friends and healers, the poets of *100 Poems and Possibilities for Healing*. Take a deep breath. Ground and center yourself in the love and passion on these pages.

We're so grateful and honored you're here on this journey with us.

Chapter 1

Open Mic Therapy: Healing at the Microphone

Laura Di Franco, MPT, Publisher

My Story

This is a BC (before COVID) story. I'm grateful to share it because I think back to the years between 2014 and 2020 and am blasted with wonder and awe about what played out before it all started. I took to the open mic stage with my poetry family, and I healed a little bit every time I was brave enough to grab the microphone (before microphones had condoms).

Open Mic Therapy is actually a poem by Grada Love. When she recited it, and I heard it for the first time, I had whiplash with the amount of nodding my head was doing.

Does the audience understand what they're doing for us? I wondered.

Now I know that most poets in those audiences know exactly what they do for a soul when that soul is brave enough to take the stage and express words they're sharing for the first time. It's more than therapy. It's authentic healing. Moments of authentic healing have endurance. They have stamina. They aren't just fleeting moments that wear off. They're moments of healing and transformation that help the individual move to another level of evolution, growth, and joy—all happening right in front of witnesses (the audience). This is powerful, vulnerable, amazing stuff.

These are life-changing moments, and I had many on those stages. I attended enough times—and was brave enough to sign that open mic list enough times—to go from shaking so hard I knew the back of the room could see to only shaking deep in my heart because I knew what I was doing was so purposeful that my soul was living its destiny at that moment.

The moments I shared a poem with others at the microphone were moments I was living my destiny—what I was born for.

You dig? Big-potatoes stuff!

"I was wondering if you'd like to be the featured poet at BusBoys in Anacostia on August 18th?"

That message changed my life—an invitation in Facebook Messenger from "Miss Kiane." You'll read a chapter by her in this book. Miss Kiane and I became friends through the open mic events, and when the message came through, I paused.

Are you good enough to be featured?

She must think you're good enough, or she wouldn't have asked you!

I typed "Yes" quickly in messenger, even with my doubt and fear grabbing hold of my chest. I've learned to deal with my purpose-driven fears. This was an invitation I longed for. One of my dreams was coming true.

Over the years, I've seen a pattern of healing in the following steps below. Jump in at any point, and you may experience a little possibility for healing:

1. Write in a journal
2. Read the words out loud to yourself
3. Share with a trusted friend
4. Share with a bigger audience (blog, social post, email newsletter, small group, etc.)
5. Grab a microphone and speak out loud

Before you read some of the spoken word poems I have to share, I want you to know something: You're good enough. You always were. This is your one precious life. Your story and message matter. What if the thing you're still a little afraid to share is exactly the thing that'll change, or even save, someone's life? It's time to be brave.

The Poems

I've written so many poems (100s in the last several years) that it was truly difficult to choose just a few for you. The ones I chose have a main message: Your worst pain or fear can be your opportunity for healing. With awareness, you get a choice. Every poem I write is channeled from a place much bigger than me. And because of that, I know they're meant for you, too. Enjoy.

What You Survived

Do you sometimes wonder
if what you survived is a test?

Like, what doesn't kill me
makes me stronger
kind of F'd up lesson-test
to see just what you're made of?

And you do survive it
looking back with a combo side-eye,
eye roll,
I'm-not-sure-if-that-was-a-cosmic-joke-or-I-should-be-stoked
kind of look.

And you move on
move forward
take the next steps
think positively in the right, best direction
resting in the closure
proud of the soul you've become as a result...

…only to wake another day
to a slap in the face
standing there stunned
looking up,
like, "WTF…
…I thought I'd been tested enough,
thought I'd been-there-done-that,
thought you'd wrung out
every last drop of my capacity
to cope on that last round."

And your mind catches fire again
when you realize
it's never the final round
until you're dead.
But for a moment you stop
and think about the score
and smile.

You're standing in the ring.

You're telling the story.

The opponent may look a little bigger this time
but the reality is
you've won every round.

EVERY SINGLE ROUND.

You lived to tell the tale
to help someone else
to take the experience
and teach
and speak
and love
and be…

…exactly who you are
as a result of your ability
to stand back up
after being knocked to the ground,
and ground yourself in the deep exhale of purpose.

YES…
YOU did that!

Congratulations, you survived.
And you will again.
And if you're wondering,
you're not alone.
Everyone's in that ring
even if you can't see it.
Everyone is struggling to stand back up again.
And there's no rule we can't offer a hand.

Let's go, warrior.
You got this next round
no matter what's thrown your way.
Training is never easy
but it's what gives you the power
to do this life with grace and ease
and a touch of badassery.
[Imagine the last stanza in the best boxing-ring announcer
voice you can muster]

"And….in this corner, ladies and gentlemen,
we have reining world champion
of the realities of life,
never give up until you die,
throw a bucket on the fire of your mind
and choose a better fight,
survivor. . .(Fill in your name).

You Were Born to Cry

You were born to cry
It's how we knew you were alive
It's not ugly, wimpy, weak
or in any way unmanly or unspeakable

If you can cry, you can laugh—both are nice.

Crying is the gift you were given
to feel, express, release, relax, acknowledge. . .
It's how we know our heart is working
how we know our soul is present
how we know something matters
It's a moment of deep healing

Happiness, sadness, unconditional love, deep grief. . .
. . . tears are the sacred, salted water we make
for every best moment.

Please cry.
It's how we know you're alive.
It's how we know we're safe to be alive with you

And if you've grown ashamed to cry
afraid
embarrassed
or stuck in conditioned meanings from the past
pause for a moment right there in that pain
for a long, patient breath
and reclaim your power in the next

You were born to cry
and laugh
and sing
and feel every single thing in the grandest capacity
All the sorrow
and all the joy

Your heart sends a flood of tears
so it can grow
so let it break, again

Don't be afraid to crack wide open

Honor your cry

Give yourself the gift of getting better at it
along with not letting that be
anyone else's business but yours
unless of course
you're lucky enough to find a shoulder
who doesn't mind reminding you that
you were born to cry.

That soul was meant to show you
just how strong you can be
and that sharing a cry means
two hearts (or more) have grown in size
and the world heals in half the time

So let yourself cry, warrior

It's okay to cry
It's how we know you're alive.

When the Sky Talks

When the sky talks
in creeping moonlit clouds,
splatter-painted stars,
and midnight hues,
I must be
the audience she sees
waiting for something grand
hoping for no finale
but an endless show.

I sit myself down
supported for hours
of upward gaze,
inhales deeper,
expectations more attached.

The sky would never
let me down.

She knows I only come
when my soul's at stake,
when I need to believe
in something more
sure.

Looking up
I feel inside
light in the dark
quiet chaos
the place I know
things fly.

When the sky talks
and she always does,
she reminds me what matters,
grounds me in magic,
tells me
one more time
that I'm more than all this
and sends me goodnight
with a kiss sweeter than
any lover.

A touch so pure
my velvet-coated dreams
sing to me
and my silvery essence
can finally rest
in her deep shadows.

The sky talks
and when I listen
more good things happen
in the time it takes
one passing cloud
to move out of view
than in a decade of thinking.

And I begin to think
I should come talk to her
more often.

Reclamation

It was an up-leveling of a different kind,
so intense I didn't recognize the signs.

The Universe always taught me the flow
spelled out what I needed to know:
the way it feels to transform
how it takes what is
and turns it into your dreams
and the life you were born to lead.

But I forgot.

Maybe. . .
. . . just maybe I prayed for it to happen this way
asked God to unlock the gate
so I could run free.
And she gave me exactly what I needed
to create everything.

It all came at once
a gift of chaos and pain
no explanation
only an answer to a prayer for my best life to arrive.
And suddenly what I truly thought I wanted. . .
. . . that well went dry.
I found myself at the bottom of a pit
so deep and dark
I didn't recognize me—again.

Damn, you did it again!

When will I learn?

You stole my identity
forced me to see a bigger, better me
the me who's actually meant
to do that dream I dreamt
once upon a time.

I thought I was her again and again.
Now I realize I had some expansion
to take on.
If I really wanted all that
I'd have to accept the fact
that there was more work to do
more fear to alchemize into fuel
a grander-sized heart and soul to grow
a more masterful circle to curate.

At this rate?
Baby, I'll be there in no time.
In fact, I've arrived today
in the reclamation of my voice
my worth
my dream
my chaos
my pain
my moment of waking
to the depth of WTF-ness
in my circumstance.

I laughed when I saw.
How could I have missed. . .
. . . everything carefully placed on the table
in front of my face
clear as day?

1. Express your love and detach
2. Set your boundaries and cast your line from there
3. Let down your hair and surrender to the sweet spot
of letting go
4. Remember you aren't supposed to know the how;
It's always a surprise and delight

The Universe's fireworks show for your soul
is not a set holiday
or size
or color
or model or make.
It's always the awe and the joy
always the feeling of yes
of ease
of love expressed
always takes care of itself
and lets itself be known

Your doubt, fear, and clench
just brace around the clarity
you spend months blocking yourself from.
If you take off the brakes and break
so be it.
If you break
and everything comes crashing down
don't you get the Divine purpose in that soul-fall
and the power that has your back?

Aren't you ready to receive the support
you always thought you lacked?
Can't you see YOU are what's holding you back?

If the stuck spot feels bigger or harder this time
it's only because you thought holding on tighter
would be the only way to survive.
Instead, that old tactic
created cement inside
and weighed you down so hard
you struggled to rise.

So dreamer, warrior, world-changer, lover. . .
. . . let go.
Break the rules.
Let the old ways die.
Birth something new.
Don't over-analyze the mess.
Confess to the blankness.
Embrace and sit in the middle of it all.
Call the angels to your side.
Reclaim what's yours.
Fly.

What's in store will happily, easily flow
like a cosmic lazer light show
showing the way to the next dance step. . .
. . . as soon as you're ready.

And girl, I know you're ready to dance.

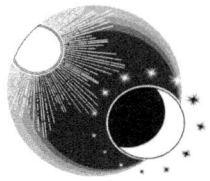

Dear Reader, now it's your turn to write! Use the space below. Don't censor yourself.

If there were no one left to upset, offend, or disappoint, I would _____.

Laura Di Franco is the CEO of Brave Healer Productions and Brave Kids Books, an award-winning publisher for holistic health and wellness professionals. Her background includes a 30-year career as a physical therapist, a third-degree black belt in Taekwondo, and 13 books (five of which are poetry). The company is celebrating its 70th Amazon bestselling title as of this publication. Laura is a performance poet and inspirational speaker, in addition to being a mom, ex-wife, and lover of dark chocolate. She and her 1000+ author community have a mission to wake the world up to what's possible. Explore all the possibilities for author-entrepreneurs at https://LauraDiFranco.com

Want to listen to some of the poetry in the book? Please hop over to Positively Purposeful Poetry on YouTube and enjoy!

Chapter 2

Crack Open Your Soul with Poetic Vulnerability

Dinahsta "Miss Kiane" Thomas, MSW, Poet, Performer

My Story

"Courage starts with showing up and letting ourselves be seen." Brene Brown

Swooping your pen across a pristine papyrus canvas with strokes of pure vulnerability is equivalent to standing center stage before a madly curious crowd gripping nothing but a towel and then releasing your grip—bare flesh and intimate parts exposed to the unadulterated opinions of friends and foes alike. The words ejected through your pen have made you both a spectacle of gossip and a portal to freedom. Finally, you are seen.

But before *they* see you, you must see yourself. What happens when the curious crowd is just a smudgy mirror with a reflection of your naked soul staring at you—pupils to pubis. Do you turn away? Do you find the finest linens to robe yourself in?

Do you create the illusion of clothes by sewing smudges together? Or do you turn around in a slow 360° spin, taking in every flawed detail, unspoken story, and uncomfortable revelation? For me, the latter is the only recourse if I want to move toward the light of healing. There have been many times I looked at my notebook page and found fragments of my inner lining staring back at me. Somehow, this poem, this journal entry, this raw reflection cracked open my very soul, and if I was willing, an adventure of self-discovery and healing was at my fingertips, literally!

One of my most vivid memories of such adventures was a poem I conceived in 2010 but did not birth until 2015! Imagine being pregnant for five years! During that time in my poetry writing career, I usually started with one line that would either be the refrain or the main idea. Then, the rest of the poem would follow! The line was, "Sometimes I feel like God is playing a real mean joke on me." Every time I said it, I heard a natural rhythm and thought this would make a great opener to a poem. I figured it would be one of those poems that sort of wrote itself, but I was wrong. Every time I sat down to write this poem, my words ran away from me, and my feelings froze up. I could feel there was a poem, but clearly, this poem was not ready to be birthed just yet. I finally stopped trying to force it.

This five-year period was filled with life-altering events and boatloads of introspection, so much so that I had trouble processing it all. I was in survival mode. Go to work. Go to church. Clean your house. Take care of your family. This seemed simple enough, but during this time, I was laid off from my job. I left the church I was a part of for the past ten years. The condo I purchased was now in jeopardy due to the loss of income. And to top it off, my bedrock, my day one, my grandmother, passed away. Concurrently, I graduated with honors in a Master of Social Work program from the prestigious Howard University. I finally landed a "good government job." And I launched my very own community-based poetry show that was gaining traction in the greater metropolitan area. For the first time, I realized that absolute joy and despair could coexist in my life at the same time. I did not know what to do with this cacophony of emotions. To sum it up, *sometimes I felt like God was playing a real mean joke on me.*

It was not until sometime in early 2015 that words began to flow. It was time to grab my pen and push! This poem was different. As the numbness slowly began to let up and the poem began to form, it was evident that my soul was screaming to be heard beyond my journal pages. This creation required another level of vulnerability. I needed to experience freedom, so I had to go all in. I had to address the pain of feeling hidden in plain sight. I had to mourn aloud my private losses. I had to tell God how I really felt. Talk about transparency! As the queries of my soul seeped from my pen, faith-filled answers followed. I emptied myself, and suddenly, there was room for hope and healing, too. Underneath the pain was a sense of survival. It became obvious to me that the crafting of this poem was not just for my own therapeutic enjoyment. Someone else needed to know that underneath their pain was survival as well.

The year I wrote the poem, I received the following invitation:

Hi Dinahsta,

Would you consider doing a Spoken Word for an upcoming event? The objective of the event is to celebrate selected individuals who. . . persevered to wholeness and now are here to CELEBRATE their SURVIVAL.

Can you say divine alignment?! With butterflies in my stomach, I agreed, knowing this was the audience for this poem. Now, you may be saying, "What is the big deal? You have written poetry before." This was the beginning of a bolder place of vulnerability. I always kept my feelings of loneliness, unworthiness, and anger to myself. I was too ashamed to let anyone know I was struggling or that my faith was shaky. In addition, I would be performing at the church I used to attend.

What if they think less of me?

What if I don't deliver?

What if it doesn't resonate?

I can proudly say that the evening was a success. Celebrants thanked me for capturing their journey in my poem. Others secretly whispered in my ear, "Me too." While others confirmed this is what I was born to do.In order to have a soul-cracking experience as a writer, it's imperative to drop the towel, see yourself, and let yourself be seen. Don't shrink in the presence of vulnerability; it's the vulnerability that will lead you to your healing. Writing is an act of courage, so WRITE!

The Poems

Hold Me

Hold me
and I shall be
Held

Like a clump of clay coddled
In the palm of a potter,
A handsy lover.
Touch me tenderly.
Spin me intentionally,
And love me creatively
Until I emerge
from your hands
a woman
Every part of my
human
Awakened.
No part kept secret
Completely clutched in your control
Every freckle, scar, and mold
Fondled by your fingers.
Every shameful story told
Caressed by your kiss.
I offer no resistance.
Hold me
and I shall be
Held

Like the fist full of dirt God used
to create the first man
I want to be
the particle of brown sand
that didn't escape
through your fingers
But rather danced in the center of your hand.
Collapsing into your strength
Whisked away by your choreography
Twist me,
Turn me,
Hold me
and I shall be
Held

Like a rib cage encapsulate
one's vitals
protecting the heart's beat,
the lung's breath,
and the veins flow.
Like a recital,
my entire insides make music
serenading the covering
that is you.

Hold me,
and I shall be
Held.

Like a poet holds a pen
Tightly grippin' the barrel
While swirls of ink
Stain sheets
Passion seeps
Rhythm, metaphors, and hyperboles

All feed the irony of the freedom found in your grasp
Agasp
My breath captive in my throat
Only to be exhaled after your poem is completed
Your words secreted
In the back left ventricle of my heart
Leaks through my pores
And gathers at my door

Hold me
and I shall be
Held.

Like Lois Lane's hand in superman's
Walking on air
All cares made small
From a posture above it all
Gulping down star-flavored oxygen
And bathing in your moon-made mist.
Sounds of exhilaration break from my lips
The super glue of your arms around my hips
Holding to this feeling of "let go"
I don't want to let go
So don't let go.

Hold me
and I shall be
Held

Hold me like a vault holds diamonds
Like a family's best-kept secrets
Hold me
Like a newborn's stare incarcerates a mother's heart
Like an Olympian holds gold

Hold me like a well holds deep waters
Like a mind hoards memories
Hold me
Like rain holds rainbows
And pain holds purpose

Just ...Hold me
and I shall be
Held.

Memory 4

So many things wrong, and
So many things right
That's that caption for the first time I recall comfort.
My brother 1, myself 4, my mother young.
Love and despair slow danced in her eyes
as she fed us both from a jar of baby food.
Old enough to cut teeth on a piece of meat,
and hold a cup of sweet red bliss with one hand,
I found just as much nourishment in the spoonful of pureed apples and peas.
Thickened by a mother's love
infused with vitamins of survival
I ate like a princess,
and comfort food never tasted so grand.

So many things wrong and
So many things right
That's the epithet on the stone above the last time I felt closeness.
It was an old fashion stroller, black as the night she pushed us through
High as the waves the moon tossed fro and to
With 4 large wheels and space for one baby to lay,

Cloaked with poverty's ingenuity,
She shaped a 1 seat convertible into a 2-kid carriage
His baby breath replaced the oxygen swirling inside my nostrils
Her ambidextrous hand drove the carriage and wiped the tears.
I was vulnerable to the elements
Greasy with Uncertainty
Yet hedged
Tethered by the pillars of I knew.

So many things wrong and
So many things right
That's the last time I knew what it meant to feel complete.
It was 1977; the 4th year of my life in Queens, New York.
The sky was a smeared chalk just over our heads
Food and shelter were interrogatives.
We wore our clothes on our backs.
Traipsing through the streets of lack.
But my 4-year-old mind only computed
the wealth of having each other.
No father, no home, no food, do direction
But we were a pack and I belonged.
It was 1977; the 4th year of my life in Queens, New York -
The last time I was complete.

No Longer

I woke up
and I
was not
AFRICAN anymore.

I no longer felt tethered to their names
No longer had to say their names
Because well my name mattered
Now…

I no longer flatlined when the Blue Light
Pulled over my black car.
I no longer flinched when *Karen*
ghost-busted the walls of my personal space.
I no longer cared if "we all got along."

I had no interest in the charred bones
hidden in Tulsa's closet
I no longer felt the water welts on my outer thigh
I no longer despised the sight of water hoses
On fire trucks sirening by.

I lost my compulsion to doodle a
Young Emmit's unrecognizable face
In my journals. Now there was white space,
And all the black smudges were erased.

I no longer felt the pinch of pain around my neck every time
I passed through underground railroad country.
Trees that beckoned to me, *Stay awhile, sit under me and let me tell you a story*
I no longer fell asleep to Araminta's freedom songs.

I no longer could smell the stench of traumatized pheromones
Choking me at the bottom of the whale's belly.

I no longer suffered flashbacks of disappearing ships
From the seashores
That I was sure
I would never see
Again.

I no longer bore the scars of a nation.

I woke up
And I
Was not
AFRICAN anymore.

Consequently,
I no longer held in my chest the heart of Genesis,
The beginning of everything black, brown, olive, red and
White.

I no longer felt the war cry of Yaa Asantewaa
gushing through my veins
pulsing beneath my skin.
No longer did I glimmer in Ghanaian gold,
The origin of Black Girl Magic.

I no longer drank from the cups of
Black Power,
Black Panthers or
Black Pride.

I no longer kept metrics like 755 home runs, 2,297 RBIs, 6,856 Bases
Hail to the Hank!
I no longer was married to the miracle of Barak,
Or the phenomenal-ness of Michelle.

I was no longer uncontrollably
possessed by the djembe
Or any syncopated sound
Like the tick tock of double dutch ropes
Or the bip bap of basketball drills.

I no longer donned divinely designed dresses of darkness
Past down from grandmothers Dorothy and Mary

I woke up
And I was
No longer……

Mean Joke

Sometimes I feel like God is playing a real mean joke on me
Like He's just laughin' at me
Throwin' tomatoes on me
See, I'm standing center stage
In a quiet, fearful rage
Waitin' on the scene to change
Spotlight shinin' bright on me
Spotlight darn near blindin' me
Yet can't nobody see me.

Can't nobody see that the make-up I wear does more than cover me
But it hides me from them judgmental stares
You'd probably give to me
If you only knew
That he beats me.

With hateful hands and a fist full of fear,
He hammers me like a rusty nail refusing to die.
He bruises me redefining the color of my ethnicity.
He buries me
Until I am invisibly free.

He beats me
With a quick kick to the gut
I'm face deep in a breathless rut
Punched between my breast
Now there's a burning in my chest
A heart set on fire
Usurping my innocence.

Sometimes I feel like God is playin' a real mean joke on me
Like He's just laughin' at me
Throwin' tomatoes at me
I'm standing center stage
Sportin' an outfit full of beige
Wishin' someone turn the page
Spotlight shinin' bright on me
Spotlight darn near blindin' me
Yet can't nobody see me.

Can't nobody see that this promiscuity
Is not just a Jezebel spirit on me
But it's the aftermath of what he did to me.
Now this "he" was very subtle
He knew that I was vulnerable
So, he preyed on me,
He watched me,
And with his poison dipped tongue he paralyzed me
Without even a struggle he forced me.
I was the woman with the issue of bloodlessness
My soul was colorless
I mean really – what kind of blood could redeem this?

Yo, seriously, sometimes I feel like God is playing a real mean joke on me
Like He's laughin' at me
Droppin' them tomatoes on me
I'm standing center stage
Trapped behind this cage
Frozen in a daze
Spotlight shinin' bright on me
Spotlight nearly blindin' me
Still, you can't see me.

You can't see past these pearly whites
Jammed in my throat is swallowed fright
Afraid that like everyone else in my life
You too will take flight
Leaving me,
Abandoning me,
Shunning me,
Throwing me
Away.
Raised Fatherless,
Left Motherless,
Forced to be Brother-less
Now I'm grown and Child-less

Images of family
All around me
Haunting me
Whispering to me
Reminding me
You've been blessed with the curse of loneliness.
Hmmm, I've been blessed...

Then why do I feel like God is playin' me?
Like maybe He's punishin' me
For things I can't even see.

Despite the legitimacy of my inquiry
Something inside of me knows that this is contradictory
To what I read in Romans 8:1-3
There is therefore now no condemnation through Christ
The one who set me free.

I'm standing center stage
Waitin' on the scene to change
But then I recall even Jesus wanting to assuage
His destiny of the cross
Praying, Father you're the boss
But I won't be mad if this bitter cup be lost.
Jesus, a lowly carpenter's son
All eyes on him to be The One
So, what makes me any different?
Spotlight shining bright on me
Spotlight darn near burning me
Turns out He was just purifying me.

I used to think God was playin' a real mean joke on me
Cause He let all these heinous things happen to me
Didn't he know these things would make and mold me
into this broken me?
Yet in His Sovereignty,
He was simply spinning me.
On his Pottery wheel he was shaping me
With his Powerful hands he was re-designing me.
Though I was marred by life's vicissitudes,
He was developing my testimony
Taking me from a tainted me to a perfect me
Singing I once was blind but now I see.

Perhaps you can relate to my story
Whether literally or metaphorically.
Maybe you were just like me--
Abused by rejection,
Violated by abandon,
Left lonely by loss of protection.

But let me serve as a reminder and point of correction
God's got some serious plans for you
Plans to prosper you,
To extract His purpose out of you,
And make good on his promises to you.

Absolutely no weapon that is formed against you
Will defeat you
All that you've been through
Serves only to remind you
That You are a Survivor!
There are no tomatoes being smeared on you.
That's just His blood covering you.
That Spotlight shining bright on you
Is just His glory illuminating you.
Know that
God ain't playin' a real mean joke on you---
He's just loving you....

Dear Reader, now it's your turn to write. Use the space below. Don't censor yourself.

Write about an inner thought (fear, concern, etc.) that you have never spoken out loud. Then, stand before a mirror (preferably full-length) and read your thoughts out loud. As you read your writing, give yourself your undivided attention.

Dinahsta *"Miss Kiane"* Thomas Author, performer, and safe space facilitator, Miss Kiane loves all things artsy. Miss Kiane's first love, however, is poetry. She has shared her work in venues both nationally and internationally. In addition to her chapbook, *Syncopated Hearts*, Miss Kiane is the co-author of a collection called *The Write Blend*, a self-help book, *The Ultimate Guide to Self-Healing Vol. 4,* and most recently, an anthology called *The Antioch Writing Retreat.* Miss Kiane uses her skills as a poet and facilitator to inspire hope, change, and healing. In her words, *"Poetry is my friend, my catharsis…my gift to the world."* To learn more visit https://linktr.ee/misskiane.

Chapter 3

Metamorphosis

Thais Conte

"A season of loneliness and isolation is when the caterpillar gets its
wings. Remember that the next time you feel alone."
~ Mandy Hale

My Story

I still remember the sweet smell and soft texture of the donut filled with
guava paste from the nuns across the street of the hospital where I was born,
in the town where I spent the first eight years of my life, my unforgettable
childhood. I never tasted anything like it in any of the many cities I lived
in and visited. I also miss the shadows of the trees where I used to play with
my friends, the trees from my grandma's house, the ones from a friend
across the street, the same ones I used to climb and cherish. Nature was
something that always brought me peace and a connection with God,

the simple and independent life I had at such a young age that I still treasure and have safely locked up inside my heart.

Years have passed, and continents I crossed before I settled in the megalopolis and cosmopolitan São Paulo, the same city I never thought I would live in; that place made me feel so small and insecure. I remember being about six years old and visiting that grey, busy, and polluted city that always made me feel nauseous. I never thought my perception of it would change a few years later.

In my early twenties, I had a chance denied to many to go to the college I chose in that enormous city I fell in love with, where I got married, had my first child, and learned to call home. I was happy, so happy and grateful until I started moving again. A whole new world of possibilities opened up to me: new friends, another child, a new culture. All of this tested my resilience, even my sanity. And here I am, more vital than ever, telling you part of my journey and my way back home to myself.

What if

What if there were no boundaries to separate us from our brothers?

What if loving one another was more potent than any religion or political position?

What if the cooperation path was indeed a two-way street, but people were always willing to do more than yesterday and pay it forward, like a new mantra, a new lifestyle?

What if empathy was the new world order and humility and generosity walked hand in hand, and we could see that every time we looked in the mirror?

It even looks like plagiarism of that famous Beatles song.

Imagine if all of this was a reality!

Imagine that together, we would make a difference, and even alone, we could take a big step.

I invite you to stop dreaming and begin acting!

Imagine that like this, dreams left behind and becoming a reality!

The Poems

Metamorphosis

Time to go.
- Let it be!
Time to move.
- Why can you just let it be?
Time to grow.
- Yet I am fine here!
Time to explore.
- But I will miss my peers!
Time to loosen up.
- Still I may need help!
Time to learn.
- Fine, something I want to do!
Time to change.
- Come on, let it be!
Time of pain.
- What's pain for you?
- Breaking the shell and moving again
Time to start.
- I can do it; I can do this!!!
It's that time again!
- Please just let it be!
- No, can't let it be!
You are constantly changing, an everlasting metamorphosis!
Time to fly!
- Finally, a butterfly!

Anywhere & Everywhere

Where are you?

- I see the ocean from my bedroom!

Where are you?

- I feel the mountain breeze on my face!

Where are you?

- I am between goodbyes, and it is nice to meet you!

Where are you?

- No, the right question should be: "How do you feel? And I feel exhausted with every move.

Where are you?

- I am stepping over sand and rocks on a cloudy day!

Where are you?

- I am in the same position as always, moving!

Where are you?

- I am anywhere and everywhere, but I feel like I am going nowhere.

Where are you?

- I am alone and don't know if I can do this once again!

Where are you?

- I am here and will always be, with my strength, my inner force, as every move brings me to a better me!

- My scars are part of me. My tears strengthened me; life gave me whatever I needed to reach my destination, where I could become everything I was meant to be!

Dear reader, now it's your turn to write. Use the space below. Don't censor yourself.

Imagine if you had made different choices in your life. How do you think it would turn out to be? Would you be willing to pay the price? Remember that one thing leads to the other, and not only good things might have come out of it, as all the good things you experienced might not have happened either.

Thais Conte was born in a small town in Sao Paulo, Brazil. Her first move was to the north of Brazil when she was eight. After that, she never stopped moving; it has been more than five countries, ten cities, and counting! She is a mom and writer with a bachelor's in Business Administration.

Find her at: https://www.linkedin.com/in/thais-conte-lopes/

Chapter 4

Unleash Your Healing Power!

Elizabeth R. Kipp

My Story

I grew up in a world of sadness, anger, and denial.

My bipolar mother was expressive, scary, bold, and prone to silent brooding depression. I never could predict when her explosive anger would erupt during the day, yet I knew it was coming. She was rife with grief over her mother's death in World War II.

"Your mother never got over her mother's death in the War," my father quietly shared one day as if to explain and excuse my mother's rage at the world. I sensed his sadness at his powerlessness to help relieve my mother's suffering.

Under all her fury lay Mother's broken heart, which carried a seemingly unbearable grief. It seemed like her grief was so deep that she was grieving for her mother, the collective loss everyone felt in World War II, and for all the ancestors who had been affected by war in any way. It's no wonder that I later went on to work in stress management, historical trauma, addiction recovery, and ancestral healing.

Mother never spoke about my grandmother and how she loved and missed her. The pain of my mother's burden inked the atmosphere of our home in a haze of darkness, yet no one ever acknowledged its presence outright. It was our family secret. No one took any action to heal the pain my mother lived with as a constant companion. I witnessed my parents slide more deeply into depression and despair. Never seeking professional help, they bore their burden silently. I saw them close their hearts in an alcoholic haze as the pain and denial ground them inexorably into hopelessness.

I saw my parent's behavior transform over time as their shoulders slumped more and more, their expressions of joy all but disappeared, and they became increasingly distant in our relationship as their drinking gradually started earlier and earlier each day.

It seemed like my parents' logic went something like this:

I'm going to pretend I'm not hurting inside. Maybe that way, it'll just go away. One more drink will help me along the way.

I lived with chronic pain for four decades, starting at age 14, before I finally healed. Unlike my parents, I had help from professionals who understood the nature of chronic pain. I learned chronic pain can be physical, emotional, psychological, or spiritual. When I healed from it, I realized my parents had suffered from chronic pain, too, but tragically never had access to the tools to recover from it.

They never had a chance at healing.

How did I get so lucky?

Suppressing, burying, or denying emotional pain doesn't heal it. It only creates more pressure around the pain, and so it grows. I learned this lesson that tragically eluded my parents.

I turned to poetry as a soothing balm. Words spread out as rhythmic waves before me, granting me entrance to undiscovered depths within me. Poetry became my private therapist, available on the spot. It emerged as a powerful and accessible tool for self-exploration, self-expression, and emotional restoration.

I encourage you to drop into your heart and let it guide your hand as it may.

Do not shrink from sadness, grief, or illness. Do not let them weigh you down. These are the very things that lead you to open your heart even further.

So, no more holding back the tears. No more hiding. All it has gotten us is that we hold our breath and hold in our emotions, and by doing so, we tap straight into disconnecting from ourselves. Enough. Unleash your healing power!

The Poems

I wrote **Katybird** for my friend, Katy, who struggled with finding self-love and inner peace. She was so lost in her isolation and sense of separation that it was hard for Katy to hear me and her friends when we told and showed her we loved her. She just seemed unable to take it all in and receive it.

Katybird

Soft whispers, Dear Sister -
I hear you crying in the night.
I promise it's gonna be all right.
No matter what has occurred, your words won't go unheard.
Soft as cotton, you're not forgotten.
Release your doubt.
It's okay. Say how you feel.
Let it reveal the pulse of life.
Oh, life is rife with struggle and strain.
Take the pain and transmute it with compassion.
Rise through those ashen remains.
Isn't it strange how we can exchange a wound for further growing,
and deeper listening to our inner knowing?
So, let the tears fall like holy rain.
Shower yourself with forgiveness again and again.
Let your heart break wide open.
Rope in love from below, above, all around.
Astound us, for you're already crowned.
I believe in you.
Can you believe in yourself, too?
Come with me to the river.
Its cleansing waters will deliver healing emotion.
Live in devotion.
Walk your path resolute.
Execute it with precision.
And get your glisten and glow on, Beautiful Soul.

Broken Bones Know How to Heal

Broken bones know how to heal.
Wild roses reveal
petals fluttering in the wind.
Yesterday, I sinned,
lost track,
went back,
forgot.
I just want to live softly.
If anything, this taught me that broken bones know how to heal.

My angst will only conceal the power and the glory.
We're always starting a new story.
Ebb and flow.
Look to the ginkgo -
resplendent yellow, mellow, and sweet.
It knows how to retreat, refusing to compete,
for it knows its essence,
standing effortlessly in presence.

Broken bones know how to heal.
The rose thorns only reveal—pain is part of living,
So is forgiving a drop of blood spilled in a prick.
Oh, the trials of life tick away one by one.
I'll not come undone because broken bones know how to heal.

In From the Cold

Come in from the cold.
Cross into the light.
You say things in your life are just getting old.
Heart feeling heavy?
Maybe it's time to bury the past,
or will you let fury send you to a bitter end?
Truth be told, you haven't sold your soul.
You just lost track of it somewhere along the way.
It went temporarily astray.
Your heart can outlast all the hurts and blows.
Have you forgotten?
You hold a light inside that shows you where to take the next step.
There's no exception here.
Just let it steer you.
Disappear your fears.
Every moment is your premiere.
It's time to expedite a new beginning.

You say your innocence was stolen,
shattered and broken.
You're questioning if you'll find wonder once more.
You say it feels pretty thin finding refuge within your own skin,
and just trying to keep yourself safe.
There's nowhere left to escape with your heart so exposed.
Can you come to the threshold and come in from the cold?

Can you believe more in mysterious magic than in such delirious tragic?
Imagine once more a passionate ecstatic in your life.
What will it take for you to shake free and forsake this vision of calamity,
and finally reclaim your sanity?

You left your soul at the bottom of a bottle.
What will it take for you to cobble it all together again?
We all sin.
It's been this way through the ages.
Even the sages themselves have to begin again.
Bravely brush your fears aside.
There's no room for pride anymore.
When will it be time to score food for your spirit?
Can't you hear it begging for more?
This human condition - there doesn't seem to be an intermission.
We're all looking for the heart to start over again.
Maybe this time you'll regain the wonder in its transmission.

Reclaim your innocence.
Life just doesn't make sense most of the time.
Paradigms shift.
Find the gift in the moment instead of allowing your worries to foment.
Let go of that inner war.
Open yourself and let love come to the fore.
Can you believe more in the mysterious magic than in your delirious tragic?
Imagine and welcome once more that passionate ecstatic to your life.

So, come in from the cold.
Turn into your light.
You don't have to treat yourself like this anymore.
Haven't you had enough of the night?
Turn into forgiving and thanksgiving.
Come in from the cold and turn into living full out.

Release your doubts.
Replace them with devotions.
Let them flow effortlessly as you swim the human sea of emotions.
Delight and hold yourself tight in them.
Discover your nobility in vulnerability.
Become your own kindred spirit instead of your biggest critic.
Gather yourself up.
Behold your light finally and come in from the cold.

Solve the Riddle

I live inside the beat of my heart.
The shape of my breath defines my art.
I color outside the lines.
It's sublime to live in the wild.
I'm not a child anymore.
Don't try and score me.
There's so much more to me than flesh and bone.
I'm not alone.
I live with the ancestors.
They're soaked into my bones.
They're holding me at the front of the line.
It's my job to complete the feats they couldn't reach in their time.

It's not serendipitous that we're here together right now.
We're caught in the magnificence.
There's no doubt how things came to be what they are.
It was written in the stars.
This time.
This sign.
I'm not turning a blind eye to the possibilities laid out like a banquet before us.
I'm not even gonna try to take it all in.

I'm not here to reject or correct.
I'm here to connect and evolve the entire system.
Give birth anew.
The ancestors always knew the potential.
They just couldn't quite move beyond what seemed essential to them at the time.
I'm here with you today to solve what they couldn't,
To evolve and break through the bonds of this system of limitation into liberation and creation.
A new tomorrow without the sorrow of separation.
Let there be no hesitation.

We're all here to heal.
Seal the deal for a new future.
Render the past obsolete.
Complete the mission started so long ago.
Come out of the shadow.
Stop tiptoeing around.
We're lost and we're found.
We're on the brink.
It's evolution or bust.
Trust the flow of the Universe.
Let the ego and its pure greed take a back seat for once.

Feel the flow.
Breathe.
Find the ease and the mellow.
Heal.
We're not here to live in misery.
Face that thing you fear.
Let it uplift you into fearless living.
We're here to beat vibrantly in the Mystery.
Let it shake you beyond complacency or the precautionary.
Connect back to yourself.
You are the possibility.
Claim your authenticity.
Awaken.
Solve the riddle.
And evolve.

Dear Reader, now it's your turn to write! Use the blank space. Don't censor yourself.

Nature's Healing: Use nature as a metaphor for healing. Write about how the changing seasons or the resilience of plants and animals can inspire your healing process.

Elizabeth R. Kipp is a Stress Management and Historical Trauma Specialist, Trauma-Trained and Yoga-Informed Addiction Recovery Coach, Ancestral Clearing Practitioner, and best-selling author of *The Way Through Chronic Pain: Tools to Reclaim Your Healing Power.* Elizabeth R. Kipp is a long-time seeker of truths with a foot in both the spiritual and scientific worlds. Her life experiences and training enable her to bridge the gap between these two worlds.

Her deep connection to the spiritual world, including her ancestors' spirits, supported her through multiple surgeries, decades of prescribed medications, and a long, persistent search for modalities to help her heal.

Now, in recovery, Elizabeth guides people to unleash their healing power. She uses Ancestral Clearing, Yoga, Meditation, and other powerful tools to help people release their past burdens and live a life free from suffering.

You can find out more about Elizabeth here: https://elizabeth-kipp.com/resources/

Chapter 5

Seeing Myself

Lisa Karasek

My Story

I was beyond frustrated. I was angry. I sat there again, beside myself, dumbfounded by what just happened, while my mind raced in a million directions. I sat there for the last time, asking myself why. I realized that it was because every try provides more details. Every try brings clarity. Every try tells my body what's real. I get more of the puzzle every time. Every fight, every tear, I'm able to return to my Self faster. I collect what I need to learn, and my emotions pull me back, assisting me in detaching from the wound, and honing in on my peace.

It was 6 am, and he was on a tangent, ranting into the space between us from the other room. In typical fashion and at full volume, he denied everything he said, denying pushing me or holding me against my will so I couldn't move, and denying any responsibility for the broken door even though it was obvious - the doorknob was broken and hanging, and chunks of wood were scattered on the floor. He went on and on about everything being my fault. "Just stop fighting with me, please," I cried. Sitting in deflation with an overwhelmed nervous system, I began to shake.

I was mad at him, yeah, but I was more angry with myself. I told myself for far too long *no more bending, you're done,* even after I promised myself so many times to never do it again, to not put up with it anymore. To not accept any more excuses or persuasions.

I've gone too many rounds like this. I've suffered a great deal of disappointment and loss. The feelings of deficiency and the void of love coursed through me stronger than ever before. That day, I was able to take all my anger and turn it into drive.

Resiliency is both a blessing and a curse. Because in the beginning everyone is awesome. There's always that point, though, when the relationship starts going in the direction of more. At this point, support always becomes an active effort on my end. My fear of abandonment wound and the irrational belief that people never choose me dictates my tolerance level for (and the need to always be) trying. I invest to create and experience what could be. I want this. I want more than singlehood. I choose this person to share and be real and vulnerable with.

The hard part comes after so many triggers, and the fighting is more than I'm comfortable with. The process of understanding that 'I'm capable but they're not' starts. I love this person, so how can I work with that? *You rose before, you can do it again* goes through my head.

I don't know about you, but I need/want connection. I need/want to feel loved. I need/want touch. I have to remind myself that I also need safety.

Choosing to leave someone because they aren't capable is hard. The love is there. In fact, that love is probably stronger as a result of the amount of compassion and empathy I gain from the experiences we go through together. I see there's a choice they can't make. But still, it's okay to say no to unwanted behavior and prioritize myself.

Once provided the time and space to recover from the toxicity, and the further away from that energy I get, I slowly start realizing in pieces how much I give away, and the passionate process of rebuilding starts. The layers I process are often put down and laid out as poetry.

The Poems

The Woman She Goes In

The woman she goes in to feel her peace
The woman she goes in to be in peace
The woman she goes in to release all her worries and doubts
The woman she goes in for the calm

The woman she goes back
Each visit bringing more clarity
Every return awakening new perspectives
Every step leading to ascension
Rising
For her to meet her truth

Have respect for this determined woman
Her forward actions are not weaknesses
But palpable measures in strength

Dutifully bound is she
To her divine internal goddess
Her return to safety
And noble and worthy stability
The climb it's not beneath her
But it is her sacred victory

Still Alive

I see you
Hiding over there in the dark
It's hard to look at what's in front of you
Too many people knocked you down
No more hits please I need a break
It's hard to feel and be You

I see You
Staying in the dark
It's safe
And comfortable and warm
But there's a shadow cast over you
And people are actually trying to find you
May I put some light on you?
Just for half of one day?
I promise it won't hurt you

I hid once too
For a very long time
I allowed all the kicking and punching to keep me afraid
But one day I saw something outside my shadow
And I was curious
When I reached for it the light brought my hand to life
Startled, I pulled my hand back
But that thing I wanted didn't go away

I sat in my shadow
Knees under my chin
My head buried in my arms
Just sitting and rocking
Intentionally blind to what was outside my dark haven

I wanted to live there
Be holed up
Numb and unrelated
But that thing I wanted wouldn't go away

I waited until night time to reach for it again
I put my hand outside the shadow
And it was once again lit up
How? I wondered
So I put my hand out and pulled it back again multiple times
Every time alive and in the light despite the dark
I tried my other hand
And both my hands
Then my foot
Every time I saw my parts alive

I rested and I slept on it
Thought about it for several days
And that thing I wanted never went away
Knees still folded
Chin in my elbows
I sat there peering and yelled at it
That thing I wanted wouldn't go away

I stood up and ran out into the light and grabbed it
Turned
And I wasn't allowed back into the dark
Like a glass wall
I pounded and I pleaded

I was kicked out from my shadow
I stood with my back against the glass wall
Barefoot and tattered
In need of a shower

This thing in my hand I clenched it
Hands heavy like weights at the end of my long dangling arms
Clenching this thing
Once in a while I raised it, opened my palm and half glanced at it
Shoulders hunched away from the glass not wanting to be there
But too afraid to release myself from it
It's tiring being on my feet for so long

The thing in my hand began to tingle
Prickly and vibrating in my hand
I opened my palm and it whirled
Like a drone or a diamond it hovered
And flew up to my face
It was shiny
And it showed me my face
I didn't recognize myself
I made a face
Then I began to cry

Suddenly my heart felt alive
Someone walked by and handed me a fruit
As I bit my ears came alive
Traffic and footsteps and city noises
They all came alive
Without consciousness I stepped away from the wall
Walking distracted looking this way and that
I felt the concrete under the soles of my feet
It was cool and warm at the same time
I moved
And I remembered
I'm alive

And so are you my love
Take my hand
I placed it in your shadow
Grab it and walk with me
I want you to know that you're alive

Dear reader, now it's your turn to write! Use the space below. Don't censor yourself.

When feelings overwhelm you, but you're not lost by them, imagine you're another figure in the room looking at you with all the sympathy and compassion a soul can hold for another. What do you say?

Lisa Karasek is an expert Intuitive Healer, TRE® Certified Facilitator, and Certified Eating Psychology Coach who is able to update her client's states of being to assist in healing. Using ancient, multi-dimensional healing and Holistic Metamorphosis®, consciousness-based practices, and TRE® (tension and trauma releasing exercises), Lisa powerfully guides her clients to a healthier, happier, more purposeful life.

Lisa is dedicated and passionate about helping you work with the dynamics of your self-relationship and believes this is the key to most Mind Body Spirit disease and illness.

Lisa offers private sessions, group coaching, group events, classes, space clearings, and more.

Service packages and memberships for healing, plus access to her classes and events are available.

Lisa is an educator, speaker, and events facilitator.

Lisa brings her many qualifying expertise and experiences to every event, workshop, program, conference, and retreat.

Mind Body Spirit Guidance, because everyone deserves an authentic self relationship. https://lisakarasek.com/

Chapter 6

Climb Coconut Trees to Cloud Mountains

Carole Park, Spiritual Chi Yoga Healer and Teacher

My Story

"You have no chance. Unless you go into fringe theatre."

Did she say that?

I saw the wide smirk on Miss Klegg's face whilst she still held my poem in her hand. My heart skipped a beat; I felt my face flush an uncomfortable rosy pink. My arms suddenly felt weak.

It took me days to write that. I thought my Sun poem was lovely!

I was a hormonal, sensitive 17-year-old and prided myself on my writing. At six years old I could read and write as well as I can now, maybe even better. I came into this world 'a natural,' or so I believed. For as long as I can remember, I was hungry to read and loved to write poetry. Miss Klegg wasn't just an English teacher; she was also the School Deputy Headmistress.

They used that title in those days. She was influential, and her harsh words echoed within me for many years.

I didn't write poetry for a long time.

I can't do that; I'm useless!

I didn't even want to read it. I remember reading Tolkien's masterpiece, *The Lord of the Rings.*

Oh, not poetry! There's way too much poetry in this book!

I skipped the poems, including all the beautiful songs the elves and nature spirits sang. Any documentaries on TV or radio about poets were immediately turned off. *No interest!* I didn't realize this was a result of one teacher's comment.

One Christmas I bought my husband a book about William Wordsworth's poetry. He wrote about the surrounding countryside, which is only an hour from where we live now. Andrew wasn't interested, but I found myself reading it and got hooked. I felt tuned into him and loved his rich nature poems. It triggered an old calling, and I began to read more poetry, even Tolkien's.

Why had I missed these before? They're wonderful!

In my spiritual practice, I love to work with Green Tara energy, and one day out of nowhere found myself sitting in front of my laptop, writing a poem about her. It flowed easily and naturally.

What's happening? Hey, look at me, I'm doing this; I'm writing poetry!

The light that flowed effortlessly when I taught classes suddenly came through as poetry. The channel was open. My whole body came alive with a vibrant tingle. I was full of energy and enthusiastically rushed outside to tell my husband:

"Listen! I've written a poem!"

"Very good."

He didn't get it but did his best to sound interested and supportive.

This was a powerful turning point in my healing and writing journey. I couldn't believe I had done it at first, but the poems continued to flow. Poetry has now become part of my spiritual practice and path. I write poetry as I experience life and write uplifting poems as gifts, especially if someone is going through a hard time.

I was inspired to write the poems in this chapter whilst on a challenging spiritual retreat in Thailand. The process was transformational and brought me a great deal of joy.

The Poems

The Magic of Coconut Trees

From scarce penetrating roots
To a thirsty nest of spray,
The humble coconut tree presents

Rising with great majesty to dazzling heights,
This magical array of nature
Rises proudly and then politely bends

Pure nature power amid humid heat,
An exotic reach to the perfect sunset
Dancing proudly in the warm ocean breeze

Long, gentle fingers with the strength of giants
Purifying the air to make way for new creation,
They collaborate with the might of the seas

Clearing away pain with the essence of life
The long figures become welcome knives
Nature's finest elements at work

Their yellow inflorescence points high
While immense bees investigate;
Their secrets wait for release into the world

Flower stems that give birth to young healing fruit
An impenetrable green shell holds the zest of life-giving water,
And gives way to a pure white sweet flesh

We eagerly consume with hungry glee,
Replacing our electrolytes lost at sea
Our deep yoga practice, now refreshed

The pretty Common Mynah Wrens visit
Accompanied by coloured tree sparrows,
Their perfect song chased into the wind

Thai faeries whirl in the floating summer breeze
Ethereal, hypnotic and mischievous
Their exotic movement, exclusive to their kind

Silver and gold, fingers and toes point and gyrate in coconut leaves,
A unique fan dance of rhythm, so uplifting
My heart opens with joy, feeling deeply kissed

I climb soaring pyramids high in the sky
As faerie radiance shines up around the spiraling mist,
This healing experience I would never have missed

Climbing Cloud Mountains

Far above the earth
We phase, through shades of candy grey,
A shimmering other world of moisture
That gives way to pillars of mystery,
As we climb the cloud mountains to heaven

Past swirling islands of capture
Revealing a sun valley in the sky,
Around rivers of the cosmos, we glide;
To a breathtaking sea of magic,
Giving way to a lake of dragon's breath

An oasis in a cascading white landscape
Opens to a lost horizon of flowing whispers
With limitless hidden depths,
Transforming into pyramids of fresh beginnings
The building blocks of life

We weave the path of faraway legends
Opening childlike fantasies,
Granting a welcome hint of faery tales,
A sweetness you can almost taste,
With a very essence that opens the heart

Soaring high above the sentient of peaks
A complex simplicity of nature appears,
Only to fall into an unfolding enigma
Of great rolling dragons, hushed,
Their secrets we may never solve

Harmonious space where dimensions and time flow
In a glorious spectacle of hope,
Where formless tai chi shadow dancers
Dissolve and bridge the arch of tranquillity,
Flowing in and out, now here, now gone

Entranced by this eternal sea of shimmering light,
Our destination, long forgotten,
We glide through this timeless place,
A slight veil over the gateway to eternity
The divine cloak that envelops the earth.

Dear reader, now it's your turn to write. Use the space below. Don't censor yourself.

Your eyes glide up to the crown of a tall tree. Gaze at the clouds. Relax, close your eyes. Watch what happens.

Carole Park is a dedicated light worker and professional healer with 23 years of expertise. She uses a blend of pure, high-vibration Ling Chi (pure healing light) energy healing and a synthesis of Tai Chi, Chi Kung, Yoga, and Meditation evolved from practice and experience. Through working with personal clients and teaching group classes, Carole developed her own Ling Chi Yoga series designed to bring yoga and healing back together. She runs workshops and seminars that involve her own insights and fusion of Vedic, Buddhist, and Taoist teachings. She gives demonstrations and presentations as well as providing one-to-one sessions. Carole helps you unlock your powerful potential, come back to wholeness, and manifest your best life. Contact her for a free consultation and personal plan today: https://goddessembodiedyoga.com/

Chapter 7

Two Sisters: One Love - A Bond to Cherish

Dorri C. Scott, MSW, Exec MBA and
Zanzel (Moma Zey) Kathy Roach, MA

Our Story

This story is about two Women. The two are sisters, albeit four years apart (Dorri is the oldest). Dorri C. Scott and Zanzel Kathy Roach share one love.

Girlfriends and "besties" on a mission to serve and give back, the sisters share a love for God and family and honor a commitment to community. Collectively, they use their words, share, and give back love in wondrous ways to touch lives and make the world better. Powerfully, the two poets use their words to help and heal and serve communities where they live.

Educators: The sisters have spent 60+ years combined from the classroom to the boardroom, teaching, nurturing, caring, and connecting with their many students ages 3 - 103. Talented and tenacious, the two speak to audiences worldwide and bring an optimistic view steeped in their faith and courageous conversations as they are social justice advocates and forward thinkers. Favorite poets who have inspired their stories include Dr. Maya Angelou (a mentor to Dorri), Nikki Giovanni, and Gwendolyn Brooks. Zanzel is particularly fond of Grammy award winner Jill Scott, the book of Psalms in the Bible, and spoken word—her own.

A classroom teacher, Zanzel is a special education teacher and continues to teach in her hometown of Passaic, New Jersey. She is a liturgy dancer at church, loves all forms of dance, and uses her melodious voice and poetry to lift others. High-spirited, she is joyful, funny to the bone, and loves to crack jokes.

Her presence in any room adds light and love. The "baby" of the family, her healing words, and poetry help others to feel the kindred support and connection she learned to give first to herself. Committed to the least of us, her healing words help others dig deep within. Having discovered the power of self-love, Zanzel, a faithful zealot, is married to the love of her life (Minister Marco) and is mother to a teacher, Vaniah Faith, also an educator. Zanzel is an animal lover and has hosted a bird, dogs, and most recently, Herbie the Hermit crab at her home. A place for all, the Roach family honors and invites all with a heart for sharing God's love.

Dorri (the oldest, and she loves saying it and especially enjoys reminding Zanzel that she is the oldest sister) is one to be reckoned with and a woman often described as "that woman." She is a one-of-a-kind woman. and beats to a drum of her own. Unique, well spoken and high-spirited, she uses a quick wit to wow audiences, lives a life of gratitude and is especially grateful to her family and friends who are with her in the journey as she is completing her doctorate in Education Leadership.

She is an educator: Dorri is the Dean of Diversity, Equity, and Belonging at an independent girls' high school in Maryland. She owns a business: Dorri is the practice manager of a mental health education services practice and a serial entrepreneur, from publishing to writing to speaking to teaching and counseling, bestselling author, and renaissance woman. She lives, breathes and loves her advocacy work to make the world better toward justice, peace and equity.

She owned her first business at age 11, which started in her parents' basement.

A book lover and life learner, "Scott's Library" was her first advocacy act toward social justice, as the library served as a bridge to help others learn and become familiar with black and brown authors, often hard to find in the late 60s and 70s. Her homemade cards with brown and black faces were an added value amongst the product offerings in the bookstore and library. A storyteller, she wrote, told stories, and shared poetry. The humble beginnings continue to propel her writing.

Having traveled to 38 countries and 44 states, Dorri uses her velvet-like voice and infectious personality to educate, empower, inspire, and inform. The survivor of a life-changing stroke, having lost the right side of her body, now fully healed, lives a life on purpose, is passionate about helping others to heal, and wholly honors her faith. Inspired by words, Dorri considers herself a "walking miracle," loves sharing stories, journals daily, uses words to help others heal and Dorri cannot dance; yet makes great movement."(It's a family joke).

The mother of two young adults, Brittany Joi and Brycen Scott, are the love of her life. With a huge heart her journey continues to be a walk of faith and healing toward healing.Witty and well-read, Dorri loves dogs and is a voracious reader who has never met a book she does not like. Simply, any book will do.

The two daughters of Leonard C. Scott (now deceased) and Cloria B. Scott (93 years and counting) live the legacy and lessons learned from their parents who courageously left the segregated south before they were born in search of freedoms denied under Jim Crow laws. They sought, looked for and found new opportunities.

The two sisters, linked at the hip, are beneficiaries of their parents' commitment to hard work, love, and faith in God.

From a homemade love shared, they exude positivity, enjoy family gatherings, honor the sister code with boundaries and grace - no judgment allowed, and see the glass half full always. The "girls" affectionately named in childhood by their parents, talk on the phone daily, continue to use their voices, poetry, words, good deeds, and wisdom to heal others toward joyful living.

Committed to your healing, the sisters recommend:

Daily meditation and prayer.

Starting with a prayer and ending daily with praise.

Keeping a gratitude journal.

Smiling.

Showing love everywhere you go.

Being a friend

Practicing grace.

Using your vision and voice to heal and help others model and make way for the power of sisterhood (and brotherhood) with gladness, thanksgiving, and kindness.

The Poems

Poems by Dorri C. Scott

That Woman, The One

Born for a purpose
Designed by God
Destined and determined
Renewed daily
She is
That Woman, The one

Gifted and inspired
She speaks truth
Whispers words of hope and healing
Daringly she believes for a better tomorrow
She is that Woman
The one
Never outworked from sun up til its done
She is on a mission
Heavy laden, not distracted
She know it takes all of us

Her heart for doing the right thing - albeit not easy
She is That Woman
The one
Steadfast and steady
Strong to the bone
Mindful and prayerful
She seeks greatness, lives it
Bestows it too

Able bodied, often tired
Her dimmed light shines
As kindness and love reigns
She is
Tender hearted and tenacious
understands her mission
Conveys the message
With kindness and a smile
That Woman, She is the one

A leader, she invites all to the feast,
Dress up, dressed down
Come one, come all
To the table of truth
Where equity abides
And grace greets al hearts
At the belonging table
Where wisdom abides
Conversions to connect
Justice rings
Joy reigns

Seats are readied
for the rich and poor
A Gathering room
Space with access
Color filled character driven
It is friendly and inviting

In search of truth,
A sacred space
To become and be
Uplifting and shifting
Hearts are changing
Realizing and recognizing
We are not that different afterall

More alike than we thought
That Woman
She Is the one
Sharing for change
Stories of the underserved
A way to honor
All God's children

Fighting to the end
Battles to be won.
Weary, never worried
She dreams
Wastes no time on words,
Instead depends on God and His good works
through sit ins, marches and writing campaigns
She huddles,
Studies, learns
listens to understand
Making sense of mayhem which continues to divide

The real meaning and message
AKA the American way
based on the US constitution
and
Bill of rights
and
The emancipation proclamation
Everyone's freedom is at risk

For liberty, life and pursuit of happiness
An allegiance to the American flag
She will never cease to struggle
For the fight that all might win

Not til the battle is over
Will she give up
As she knows there is STILL
Work to be done
For

Voting rights, climate change
no bans on books
women's rights, poverty be gone.
She is That Woman, the one
Expecting and inspecting
For immigrants
The insane and insecure
And locked up, persons
Too many locked down wrongly accused
America got a mental health crisis
Shame be gone
Haters stop hatin'
Liars stop lyin'
Racism No more
Today we rising
With a new faith
We fast forward
From our ugly beginnings
To here and now
With fortitude
Fearlessly
To the bitter end
Embrace empowerment
Speak out
Say it aint so
That others
See the good in our land and
A people seeking
Songs of hope
Sing it loudly
That freedom might ring
Freedom for all
For the legacy of our children
And a better tomorrow

Breathe

Supplied, undenied
life is delivered daily in small
bites
For the taking
B R E A T H E

Over with it, done with that
Let it go
Choose
You are not alone
B R E A T H E

A Leader in your own right
Follow and flow
Know when
to call for help through the
storm
the one you can depend on
-what makes sense for you
B R E A T H E

Honor solitude
Trust and take time
Healing in progress
It's a process too
Go slow
B R E A T H E

Speak softly,
Take it easy,
Say it ain't so
(when it ain't)
Let go. Let God
B R E A T H E

Pleasing others is over
Remain diligent
Never wane
Off the merry go round of
insanity
And feeling insecure
You are thriving
B R E A T H E

More than
Giggles and games
You have learned through it all
Smart cookies don't crumble
B R E A T H E

Enjoy the message
Live the lessons
Go far
Applaud your wake up call
B R E A T H E

As rising aint easy,
Daily choose wisely
You are the best of the best
Never quit, don't stop
B R E A T H E

Don't miss the window
Which will close if you're not
careful
Be mindful of messiness,
Memories and messages

People and places
who came to distract
Cause they lack,
Know they
Never had your back
They want what you do
what they can't
who they ain't
B R E A T H E

Live your truth
Be that one
Who cares, dares and dreams
Stand alone in the dark
Be awakened by the light
B R E A T H E

Letting go life will show you
Everybody was not intended
To be your friend
Sliding and hiding
Inwardly crying
You played the game
Their way
lost your soul
Stopped breathing
To the rhythm and rhyme -
YOURS
In search of another's garden
Never for the taking
You were faking
Holding on, clinging
for what?

Hoodwinked and hurt
Only to discover
You recovered
Da' truth don't change
B R E A T H E

Reminded by the ancestors
Their whispers and words
Momma knew, Daddy too.
Sister spoke, Brother clued you
in
Game's over.
You are healing
Live on
B R E A T H E

Kitchen Talk

There be something
'bout the kitchen
that presses upon her
enables and empowers women worldwide
To let it go,
Be loose
Get down
Speak n' share truth
Be happy and nappy,
Sad or glad
Straight no chaser
Hot and heavy
No holding back
Out loud, if she wanna
Women understand and know
Kitchen TALK is her way
And woman wise

A sacred space shared by sisters;
all races and religions,
cultures and colors
Kitchen Talk
is conversations and connections

The heart of the home
With friends and family
Kitchen talk at tableside is the place
A high-spirited experience
Understood world wide
Women get it
Her sacred space and
gathering place

where talk in the Kitchen
Sanctified and sanctioned
Hummed with an Amen
Added to
Can I get a witness?
It is now and forever every woman's truth

Kitchen talk ushers in all
Puts some out and lets in if you think you belong
It is
Talk about men,
how he walks that walk
in a cool suave sexy way,
Mr. Cool- he so smooth
Or the rapper with words
make you wanna holla
drop it like its hot
He got game,
Knows your name
He sexy and strong
A lot of trouble and no good
He chases to please
Again he aint no good
But you give in anyway
He so fine.
She believes the lies
he been telling
house to house
too long, too mich

The man everyone loves and hates
You better ask somebody
When you 'gon start loving yourself?

"Girl"
"We all know, He ain't no good"
From steamy nights and somebody elses'
To secrets never to be shared
Take em to the grave,
Don't let your secrets kill nobody.
Grown women know
The sage of the circle
Tried to tell you
As
Kitchen talk takes no prisoners
especially talk 'bout Ms. Thang
Riding all over own in her new
Black on Black BMW
With her big self in that too tight dress
Showing chest and too much flesh
"I cant staaand her."

"Mmmhhh"
Kitchen Talk
Girlfriend to girlfriend
Mommas and daughters,
Sisters and Aunties,
Yentas and In-laws
Family and friends

Women be talking

Unlike the living room or bedroom talk
Kitchen talk is real
Where everybody and all things
Are equalized, embraced and endured to the end

Even those who are dignified,
educated, bourgie, broke,
down town,
up town, city side or countrified
All come sit table side
To get on down
With Kitchentalk
For sake of the sisterhood

Cause talk about mommas mean greens,
Bubby's chicken soup
Aunt Juicy's homemade 'nanna pudding and
Granny's lemon cake
Brings every body back home down to earth

"Ooooh chile'"
"What you say?"
"Stop playing"
Stop playing"
"I cant take no more, Lead me to the door"
"No Say it again, say it again"

Kitchentalk at tables side
Passed down generation to generation
One woman to another
Words of wisdom
Food for thought
A few lies here
The circle and sisterhood
Friends having fun
Sharing secrets and sometimes a side eye
Speaks even when the words don't say a thing

KithenTalk is real
It be happyand nappy
Holla if you wanna
The heart of the home
with friends,
Sometimes she be alone
Women love her some kitchen –
As in
KITCHENTALK

Grab a seat, warm it up
Hold my seat
Eat, Be merry
Hair fry, fish fry
by herself or not

KITCHENTALK
is a connection
hers, mine, ours.
life ways, wisdom
other women's business
-Yours too

Mommas and their daughters,
Sister, Aunties, Godmammas and Yo' girl
Eating
Beans and burritos
Lasagna and lamb
Pork and sauerkraut
At Momma's table
On New Years Day
Always on Sunday
Joined by the gospel bird
Kitchen Talk brings everybody back home

It is the equalizer
Grown folks know
No men allowed
Ushered back to his man cave
after he was caught peeking

Kitchen Talk Is her place
where she go cause she know
Sharing is caring and
No Men allowed

Kitchentalk
comes from the soul
The core of one's being
And it don't get much deeper than that
It is a state of mind
For laughter and tears
Sharing fears
Screaming jeers

Sisters, Besties, Yo girl, Kin
and even the one you can't *staaaand*
winds up in the kitchen

Passed down for years
Generation to generation
one woman to another

Words of wisdom
Food for thought
Sayin something
Talking loud
Acting up
Being herself wholly
A woman's way
Kitchen Talk is really getting down

Poems by Zanzel Kathy Roach

47

I can tell I'm getting older
By the way I get out of bed
I use to just jump up
Now I roll out instead
When I get up in the morning
To put my feet on the floor
Sit for a minute
B-4 I stumble to the door
Gravity has my body sagging a little
Especially in the middle
Now I make a list or note
4 everything
Can't remember quite as much
So I rely on paper -n- pen
To keep in touch
My next whip will be
Soft leather equipped
Easier to step out
A senior gave me that tip
Hot flashes ride my body
Like an escalator
Night sweats wake me up
Reason why I keep ice water
n a cup
I can tell I'm getting older
Don't converse as much
To people anymore
No explaining or hanging
On to chit chat

Squash that at the door
Know what I want
Go 4 it and concentrate
Never mind my age
It's never 2 late
Stay on my grind from 8-2-3
Picked up a side gig
At the University
Professor is who
I be
Spit my pieces out
Like a slow fire
It's the hip-hop in me
Keeps my youth
For when I retire
I can tell I'm getting older
By the thoughts
Running through my head
Spirit, moral, and integrity
Is the way I'm led
Don't take 2 much advise
From anybody under the age 50
Especially if their eyes are shifty
47 is my on earth living like heaven
I embrace this # with grace n pride
Found some more gray hairs
I refuse to hide
I can tell I'm getting older
By the way

I get out of bed
These minor changes
Nothing I can't handle
It's the love of the
Lord
That's my stead

I Love You

U hurt me
As a result I
Stuffed my tears
4 - 44- years

Perfection and staying
Always in control
Were my #1 goal
Projects and tasks
Is my butterfly bask

No longer will your energy
Entrap me
I'm starting with forgiveness
For the first time
I looked in the mirror
Eye 2 Eye
And spoke from the heart
"I love you"
And that's no lie
That statement was 4
Me, myself, and I

How dare I not try
To connect
Beauty, Spirit, and Joy
The days of being coy
Are no more

I'm bolder, wiser, and
Gorgeous now
Still under construction
When the curtain is lifted
The reaction will be
WOW!!!

Faithful

Be faithful until the end
The end of life
Whether sister single
mother or wife

Be kind as far as
You can go
Display kindness
Weather emotions are
High or low

Be a good solider
You signed up
By faith
When you believed
Don't murmur or complain
Carry out every order
With grace not blame

Don't be a
Whimp, punk, or procrastinator
Endure hardness as a good
solider
Do and remember
All the commands the
Lord told yah

Take it beyond this life
And live in the super natural
Forget you're being over looked
Remember the Lord
Sees and watches
Over yah

He watches over His Word
And has your name
attooed in His hand
Covers you with a shield
Of favor
As you walk this land

This is just practice
He's got your placeprepared
It's up to you
On how you wanna live
Inner court, outercourt,
Or beyond the vail

So what, you're talked about,
Misunderstood and they do you wrong
Go back and thank them,
Bless them, and pray for them
Those actions put you
Where you belong

It hasn't been easy and
It wasn't said that it would be
But He did promise
Peace, green pastures, strength, and joy
for you and me

So don't give up now
Nor wipe the tears when they
fall
Theirs a bottle under your chain
To collect them all

Be faithful until
You are called home
Whether sister, daughter,
Young man or child

Carry out each command
Worship when you don't know
What to do
Trust the words in
The Word of God
And embrace the renewed mind
Transformed in you

Way

It's okay 2
Whatever they say
I'ma still do it
The Lords way

The Lord gave me the vision
To carry it out
It's another chapter
In my life
Not a fight but a bout

Sometimes I'm challenged
Then I refresh
By going inside
That's where I hide
Not from myself
But from pollution and pride

Inside is courageous, strength,
and beauty
Inside is power, spirit, and
My call of duty

Inside is color
Water peace and sand
Inside is insight
And like the Lord asked Moses
What's in your hand

The moral of that story
Is to use what's been given
Find your purpose and
Reason for living

So it's okay 2 whatever
They say
You count the cost and
Do it the Lord's way

Dear Reader, now it's your turn to write. Use the space below. Don't censor yourself.

What is sisterhood to you? Who is your go-to, ride and die? State her name and what she means to you.

Dorri C. Scott, *MSW. Exec MBA* and doctoral candidate is an educator, mental health professional, and founding publisher of The Virginia Woman Magazine, serving 100k readers. Committed to social justice, diversity, equity, and belonging, she is a certified diversity trainer, best-selling author, and advocate for change committed to the eradication of racism, sexism, and all forms of hate and antisemitism. A voracious reader (any book will do), she enjoys reading, traveling, writing, yoga, and summer visits to Martha's Vineyard. The mother of two young adults, she resides in Washington DC, loves animals, and journals daily.

Dorri holds a BA in Political Science, a Masters in Clinical Social Work, and is a graduate of the Harvard Business School. Completing her doctorate in Education Leadership, she is writing her dissertation on "The growing banned book controversy in US schools and libraries of banned books in American schools."

https://www.dorricscott.com

Zanzel (Moma Zey) Kathy Roach's writings are inspiring, uplifting, and charismatic. She is a woman of faith, a poet, educator, published author, and a spoken word artist. Her words of hope have captivated audiences from the NAACP, City Halls, Universities, High Schools, Elementary Schools, Events throughout the United States, Local Churches, and Nonprofit Organizations. She has been featured on a blog, Seriously Maybe.Com. Zanzel has produced a spoken word CD that accompanies her book entitled "Something Beautiful," a look at life through poetry.

She finds joy and comfort in the presence of the Lord and with her family. She is known for having a way with words with a purple pen as an artist selects colors to paint a picture with a brush. She hears the melody of each word that is expressed, and will continue to write and tell her story like her ancestors did from glory to glory.

Chapter 8

Poetry as a Therapeutic Tool for Integration

Christine Falcon-Daigle, MFA, Global Sisterhood Circle Facilitator

My Story

Confined indoors by air quality so hazardous it made my eyes, nose, and throat burn, I felt trapped. Even with all the windows and doors sealed shut, the charred stench of wildfire was nauseating, compounding the ever-present sense of danger brought on by the global pandemic. Nothing relieved my headache.

The view from my bedroom window that morning was apocalyptic. Thick smoke blocked out the sun and turned everything a sickening orange hue. I couldn't even see across the street. *Is this Armageddon?*

It was September, harvest time, and typically California's best weather. Six months into the shelter-in-place order, my farmer husband—considered an *essential worker*—hadn't slowed down. He strapped on a respirator and left at dawn every day, taking both dogs with him. N95 masks were in short supply, and the public was asked to leave those for healthcare workers on the frontlines. For the first time in my life, I spent extended periods of time in complete isolation.

Earlier that week, my employer of nearly a decade lost its Napa Valley retreat center in the devastating Glass Fire. Less than 24 hours later, a beloved member of our local community died in a head-on collision.

Some were calling this surreal nightmare *The Great Pause*. As Covid-19 swept across the globe, planes were grounded, and plans were canceled. Weddings were put on hold indefinitely, and funerals were not permitted. I watched friends who owned small businesses close their doors; many couldn't afford to pay rent. Every day, we watched as numbers of new cases rose, along with the death tolls. We hadn't seen my parents for months.

Two years earlier, Mom's first cousin was killed by the Paradise Camp Fire, the deadliest wildfire in California's history, and she worked tirelessly to have Isabel's remains identified and sent to San Francisco to be buried in our family plot. At least that gave her a focus while Dad baked loaves of sourdough. We met with other family and friends via Zoom and FaceTime.

Back in January 2020, news that we'd be moving to a new home caused a major rift with our 17-year-old daughter, who was not happy about it. Quarantined at her dad and stepmother's house a short distance away, navigating high school online, she nearly stopped communicating with us. That same month, I learned I had another older sister—the second time I was surprised by this type of news as an adult, the first being some thirty years earlier—and it reopened a wound.

After the murder of George Floyd in May and the ensuing protests, one of which my daughter marched in, I began having nightmares that woke me and my husband without warning, always with me crying, screaming, and gasping for air. I was overwhelmed by a sensation that I couldn't breathe.

I began having panic attacks again, then flashbacks and intrusive thoughts related to my ex-husband fighting me in court for sole custody of our daughter. Scared to go to sleep, I wandered through our house at night. *We've gotta get out of here.* An obsession to flee had me gathering my family's passports, researching other countries in which to live, and making plans to move. I worked remotely for the first few months of the shutdown, but by June, I was exhausted and recognized I couldn't perform my duties. Full of shame, I called my boss.

"I'm so sorry, but I think I need to take a leave of absence or something."

She responded with compassion while I cried into the phone and offered to help get me the support I needed. Together, we decided I would go on disability.

My doctor diagnosed me with complex PTSD. No medication was prescribed, but group and individual therapy was. Besides our cat and my cell phone, the only things I had to keep me company were the support of those Zoom appointments, an ever-present grief, and the ache of loneliness from forced social distancing.

About this time, something inside of me kicked in—a part of me that had been asleep for far too long came back online. *This is how you endure: turn off the news, focus on your mental and physical health, work in the garden, and write.*

ABOUT THE POEMS:

This is precisely the time when artists go to work. There is no time for despair, no place for self-pity, no need for silence, no room for fear. We speak, we write, we do language. That is how civilizations heal. –Toni Morrison

Inspired by Toni Morrison's quote, I wrote the following four poems at the beginning of the pandemic. Three of the four, along with others written over the following two years, make up a chapbook of poetry I self-published in 2022 entitled *Poems from the Darkside of the Pandemic.*

The Poems

The Reckoning

I.
For far too long, I've navigated the shallows of my own grief.
Now the rising tide of the pandemic
has sucked me way out, beyond the reef;
beyond my own disbelief
into fathomless open waters,
humanity's collective grief.

I brace as wave after wave of trauma strikes,
a tsunami of intergenerational pain,
the stain of slavery, theft of bodies stolen from one land,
and theft of land from other bodies,
from those who called this land their home, millennia before me.
Spirits rise from watery graves
slave ships sail through centuries' mists
reframing the story – *his* story – from that of a nation
founded on democracy to that of a nation
founded on fear, built by domination.

Not only did my boat capsize
it was torn asunder and I
went under.

Now, it's sink or swim.

Bodies are everywhere.
Some will surface. Some will not.
We must keep swimming.
Do whatever you can to stay afloat.
Stop drinking yourself into oblivion.
It will only increase your odds
of drowning.
Ellen Bass calls this weight an *obesity of grief.*
Resist the urge to sink, to drink.
Lighten up.
Lift off.
Expand into particle and wave.
Save your soul.
Drink the Kool-Aid.
Raise the vibration.
Tune-in and find
the new frequency
inside.

Businesses are going under.
Hospital beds are in short supply.
No health insurance
No relief
No more stimulus checks—
the mailbox is empty.

Wake up! No one is coming to save you.
This is not a drill. The house is burning down!
The world is crumbling.
Embers flying everywhere, no water and
we aren't even into fire season yet.
We're sitting on a tinderbox
of rage – grief's molten hot underbelly.
Our nation is armed and mentally unstable.
Nothing can extinguish these flames.
Prepare for total annihilation.

II.
There will not be enough armed forces,
federal agents to deploy
as America's sons and daughters storm the castle.
Have we learned nothing from Marie Antoinette, or Mussolini?
Things never turn out well
for dictators and Fascists.
Try as they might to save themselves, in the end,
the bunker is always stormed,
the compound firebombed. Remember Waco?
For god's sake: the twin towers have already collapsed!

It began a long time ago
but we were too numbed out
overworking ourselves into oblivion,
caught in the trance, a dance of survival
living paycheck to paycheck
just to make rent
just to keep a roof over our heads.
Many failed at that, and we just stepped over them,
in puddles of piss, hair unwashed
we
stepped
over them
lattes and cell phones in hand.
We judged, we avoided. We didn't stop and think:
There, but for the grace of God, go I.

And now we're in deep
well past the tipping point.

Do not go back to sleep.

How to Save the World

Wait.
Did you forget something?
Your keys? Your phone?
Your original home -
A star 26-times brighter than our own
Sun?

Did you forget
To buckle in?
Mask up?
Empty your bladder?
Grab some water?

This is not a race.
Erase the space between you
and me. We are so much more
alike than you might think.
One blink and it's all up in flames
The names of the murdered, forgotten.

Did you forget something
About balance?
About presence?
About kneeling down
To kiss the ground –
your mother?
YES, Earth.

She gave birth
to all this.

You forgot something:
Your voice,
Your power,
The parts of your soul
They stole,
Tried to stuff down a hole
Like a dismembered body no one
Would ever find.

Let me remind you:
We are all one body.
Not *nobody.*
Not *some*body.
God's body.

Light-filled
Lift off
Ascend to higher
Dimensions
Let the heavy carbon footprint
Sink, sort itself out
'Cuz we got work to do.

There's always been a battle
Raging. This Age of Aquarius
Bears the burden of
Unearned privilege.
The lifting up now about putting out a hand
Pulling up a brother, a sister, your mother
So we can *all* rise.

It's climbing the mountain in spirals
No giving in, no going back
But you may rest.

Sit down on the ground
Listen to the sound of water flowing
Blue glaciers melting,
ice releasing energy
Frozen for lifetimes.

Did you forget something?
About laughing and crying
And losing control? This whole thing
A wellspring, life's creation
To keep herself company.

There is no finish line.
No first or last. Each breath a death
And on & on it goes.
Who knows?
Maybe we all forgot something –
that gold ring without end
or beginning.

No one is winning.
This is all a hoax.

A kaleidoscope
of cosmic particulate
and wave. Save yourself.
And in doing so,
save the world.

Peace!

Dark Goddess

It doesn't have to be the blue iris,
sometimes it's the dandelion, its bright yellow head
bursting from the crack between pavers.

The tenacity of life astounds me.
The way the jungle overtakes a pyramid
or an old junker is lost to the swamp.

She will never be kept down,
that Dark Goddess of Creation,
out of whose womb everything is born.

I've been longing for silence, for the embrace of night.
The quiet simplicity of those days when I would
take myself on retreat at the beach,
when my daughter was a tiny tot.

I'd choose a cozy little cabin by the sea,
something close enough that I could walk the beach
twice a day.
I loved being offline, no cell phone, no Wi-Fi,
just me, my bag of favorite books,
woodstove and groceries for a week.

I feel a desperate yearning these days
of over-stimulation, over-commitment, over-doing
a million different things
an endless to-do list and tasks to complete.
I long for candle, paper, pen,

a warm cozy blanket and soft place to land.
My soul is missing herself.
My well needs replenishing.
How do I explain this to those hungry mouths
demanding to be fed?

Close your eyes. Dive inside
reside in the deep splendor
of your own divinity.

How did I even learn this?
As a child, by staring at the stars
        out my bedroom window,
in the safe company of trees,
gazing into fire.
This is my safety, my sanctuary, my Source.
This place, my one true home.
No one can come between us.
No one will stop Her from blooming again
        and again
                and again.

She will not be silenced
or forced into submission.

Every miraculous flower and sprout
bursting through concrete *proof*
of her defiant warrior nature.

Remembering

We have forgotten who we are.

At these times, it is critical
To dance and sing, make love, break bread, *bake* bread
because the process reminds us
of our capacity to rise.

We must kneel down, kiss the feet
Of our parents, our children, each other –
Our Earth herself – give thanks and praise,
for they are *all* our teachers.

Pop a cork, drop the top,
Let the wind tangle your hair.
Feel how wild and free you truly are.

We must *kiss the book* as brother Moses says,
treat each thing we do
As a sacrament: pulling weeds, washing dishes,
even scrubbing toilets – especially the toilets,
holiest of acts

Have you ever wondered where you come from?
Why you were born: YOU. HERE. NOW?
Have you found your passion? Not the thing
that you thought you should do,
but the thing that sets your soul on fire?

Have you stopped to consider
how you ever made it this far?

How you survived
without getting killed? Arrested? Abducted by aliens?
How did you not fall off the edge of that cliff,
The one you were so hell-bent on getting to?

Perhaps you're like the catcher in the rye,
one of the ones keeping the rest of us safe?
Some cosmic goalie, blocking us from our own worst selves?
Holding us in the safety net of your arms -- the same arms
that bake bread, pick grapes, scoop poop, fold laundry?

Maybe you're one of the ones who picks up random hitch-hikers
       —all of their baggage too, even their itchy dog—
Offers them a ride, *at least as far as* you're going,
let them fill your clean car with scent of unwashed-for-weeks,
force on them a crisp, neatly folded bill, curl it in their hand,
and when they lift their eyes to meet your gaze,
maybe even hold both cheeks between your palms,
say *you are beautiful, you are loved*, and, in doing so,
remind you both who you – we – really are.

Dear reader, now it's your turn to write! Use the space below. Don't censor yourself.

In the wound lies our medicine. What is your wound, and what is your medicine?

Christine Falcon-Daigle was born to feel the unexpressed emotion in her family of origin, which she channeled into poetry from a young age. A natural storyteller and spiritual seeker, her greatest passion involves supporting others engaged in journeys of self-discovery and personal transformation. She is a published author who's worked in radio and documentary film; a Baptiste Power of Yoga instructor; a facilitator of writing and women's circles; and holds certificates in Horticultural Therapy and CTIP (Collective Trauma Integration Process). Christine resides in the San Francisco Bay Area, where, for more than a decade, she has worked for The Hoffman Institute, supporting adults engaged in experiential healing retreats. In 2023, she began collaborating with others engaged in the healing arts to offer unique, daylong writing retreats for women. She is a wife, mother, daughter, sister, and a lover of all things wild and free. Find out more at http://christinefalcondaigle.com

Chapter 9

Honor Thyself, Heal Thyself

Guy Kilchrist

My Story

Mom and Dad, why did I never get my say in what I thought and felt?

Avery points to a childhood with parents stuck in their own mess for never developing the confidence to express inner thoughts and conflicted emotions and receive feelings of love. Instead of a *joie de vivre* (joy of life), fear and sadness prevailed, leaving a trail of unfulfilled moments, grief, and fractured hearts.

Avery's grief does not age like fine wine. It festers and morphs acidic. A smile and pleasant façade belie the shame and fear of intimacy. Perpetual victimhood is Avery's alibi and addiction.

Transcending grief is like taking small sips of fine wine, experiencing the complexity of its notes, and then letting it go. Feeling what needs to be felt and speaking what needs to be said without oppression invites the gradual release of victimhood's addictive power.

Embracing grief calls for self-kindness while allowing it space and time to unfold its wisdom. This embrace doesn't erase past events but holds the potential for a profound transformation in how we perceive ourselves, others, and the world in which we live. Complete acceptance and honor of who I am (wounds, warts, and all) and what comes in life cultivates insight to overcome a debilitating fear of what others think.

We are more than our thoughts, feelings, and judgments of good and evil. The first step is challenging one's self-referential ego as the final arbiter of truth. It is not. Honoring self rather than being critical and judgmental allows one to lovingly entertain one's shadow and seek its hidden relics long repressed. Opening one's soul to a compassionate ear is a prescription for processing emotional burdens and begins to repair the harm done. This soul-to-soul reconciliation is a healing gift to humanity.

No one chooses the parents who brought us into this world, yet one of the greatest gifts we receive is their model of how to live and, equally, how *not* to live. It's a package deal. We don't get one without the other. We've earned the freedom to choose what *not* to carry forward. This is the good we are called to be. To identify oneself in perpetual victimhood throughout life is a childhood aversion to facing the sometimes-brutal truths of human existence.

It takes a leap of faith to embrace one's complicated past not as blemishes but as threads of grace to be woven into wisdom. Trusting in grace that operates "as it is" rather than how one "wishes it to be" surrenders the ego's need to control and rationalize.

The following four poems are in sequential order and serve as lampposts and willful intention of honoring self and reconciling the personal harm done to us by others and harm done to others by our own hands. It is hard work.

The Poems

Trench Warfare

The little devil
whispers, *be happy my way*
Angel mutters no
Instead, my way, the high road
They battle on to no end

Men and women both
act from deep primal urges
There's no escaping
the battlefield our souls play
Until shadows meet the light

At day's end, lay not
afraid nor burden heavy
If not, sit in the
fallow field bidding its time
Nourishing in its silence

Speaking the Unspoken

Sift hidden relics
forgotten in guilt and shame
A double-edged sword
Knowing only how to cut
keeping the blood flowing red

Secrets forgotten
Hidden to all but one's soul
Awaiting the light
to open its chambers wide
for the compassionate ear

In darkness revealed
a tender light wipes away
burdens too heavy
Accepting one's dark and light
a sacred act of courage

The Harmed and the Harmer

Step in the shoes of
other, seeing through their eyes
Stand in their shadow
Inhale their air, bear their cross
Touch the cracked vessel, and yours

Fragments of hidden
pain awaits the master's hand
To heal and make whole
souls wounded by life's journey
In our hearts lay the power

Acknowledge the pain
No façade, and no ego
Hidden hearts ascend
to reconcile true-self with
Beloved, one and other

Absolution

Accepting nothing
less than where Wisdom flows and
where shame meets its Grace
and where eyes can see no guilt
A victimhood cannot spawn

Chambers of remorse
collapse under their own weight
The sacred release
of soul's burden to carry
which it never intended

Live as life-giver
and never a destroyer
Beloved's Spirit
The sacred mystery to love
We all journey to our end

Dear reader, now it's your turn to write. Use the space below. Don't censor yourself.

Are there moments from your past that you find challenging to reflect on because they bring up feelings of shame or anger? How can you begin to make peace with those moments?

Guy Kilchrist

We are endowed with a creative and generative spirit. Sometimes, it is inspiring and beyond words; other times, it is not. Either way, it is worthy of being nurtured, not hidden.

My life is an exploration, sometimes serious, sometimes playful. My curious and creative Spirit, along with a desire for the community's common good, is the undercurrent of my life. I feel most alive and amazed when my creative Spirit is active and at play.

In life and art, I desire to maintain loose boundaries of inquiry, exploration, imagination, creativity, and service, striving to be open, honest, and heartfelt with myself and others. To cooperate in Grace, the life-giving Spirit of it all – to take me where it wills.

I am overjoyed in family, fatherhood, and sacred friendship. And most relaxed when my life's pace is five mph slower than the speed limit.

https://graceinarts.com/

Chapter 10

Being Overwhelmed and Doing It Anyway

Stacy Belinsky

My Story

One morning, I woke up from a dream, not remembering anything except the idea "to empower women."

As vague as it was, I brought up my idea during a local startup meeting and was encouraged to participate in another event, "Pitch Zoo," as one of the "pitchers" (presenters). The idea of speaking in front of a group made me feel nervous. A way that helps me get through that is by including friends, and at the time, I asked everyone who I could think of to be there. We had around 30 people in the audience, filling up the room.

Following the pitch, the audience could offer suggestions or ask questions. A woman in the audience mentioned Mothership: Hackermoms, a creative space for moms (loosely defined) and their families. This turned out to hit the general point of my pitch and also pulled me into the maker world while I explored creating a community called Hacker Gals. The original version was in my local area, and from connecting to a maker space about 60 miles north, I created a second version through that group, too.

Everyone involved had a talent or passion to share. My job, then, was to coordinate and not always be the lead for presenting. The workshops were as fun as learning to line dance and as uplifting as Gals Picture Day for professional photos.

Today, I continue to be a part of the local maker and startup creative community. Although Hacker Gals doesn't officially exist anymore, it's important to me to empower and support women. In my experience, maker spaces tend to be male-dominated, with many women joining because their husbands did. The women may be as or more creative, yet don't tend to be regular participants.

One of the newer members at my local maker space is an exception to this. She joined on her own and has many projects with deadlines that bring her in every open day. Recently, I stayed longer to hang out with her, even after my tasks were completed. We were the only ones in the building for most of the evening. "Having you here really helped me today," she said. "The conversation really helped me," I replied.

A few other members were willing to work at helping to resolve one of her project challenges before they left. I refer to this as the Serendipity Spot. It's more than paying dues. It's the willingness to participate by asking for or assisting others when asked and caring about the person, even when your interests may not match. Whether or not I created the event, I love watching the magic unfold.

Even though the basic physiological needs such as food and shelter were covered while growing up, I didn't feel supported to follow my interests. Sometimes, it was still allowed and left open-ended, such as being on the musical theater crew and having to find a ride when the group utilized a different high school during my freshman year.

I feel like I don't know what I don't know until it comes up in a conversation, such as with maker friends.

That knowledge and support wouldn't expand without my willingness to engage as a member of the community.

If I can help to relieve anyone else's stress to experience it less than I have, I want to do that when there is mutual support.

The Poems

The Life We Mask

Wearing a mask
Has such a shame
"Are you sick?
Do you always follow what's proclaimed?"

"No," I say. "I feel more protected
and safe.
You have to start somewhere."

I understand people want to follow
their own rules.
Does that mean laws don't exist?
That we display to discourage the
fools?

Do you mean what you say?
Your actions show what's true.
You seem to want one thing
And yet don't follow your own rule.

Take off the mask,
the ones that are not physical.

Take off the mask,
if it means seeing you.

Take off the mask
that hides your fear.

Take off the mask
that shows how you sneer.

Take off the mask
that has kept you disconnected.

Take off the mask
Let me see you FULLY unprotected.

It's more than the physical mask on your face.
You're hiding years of
unworthiness, depression, anxiety,
and shame.
You've buried yourself so far and deep
That you've forgotten yourself.
There's not even a little peak.

You've mastered being a chameleon
And getting through life so far.

Where is the true person?
Why is the mask so hard?

Following others' examples
got you through.

Following others' examples
made you seem cool.

What the mask is hiding
is the person who you want to be.

I know you're there.
I know you want to be free.

What will you risk?
What will you do?

I'll be here.
Waiting to see you.

The Black Hole

I always want to express
More than you are willing to bear
So notifications are cleared
As soon as they appear

What if I did it
as a conversation with myself
and stopped chasing behind
those who want to stay on the shelf?

Would it be as satisfactory?
Would I find a way to find my tribe?
Cause this is nonsense
And I do it to myself
All I really want to do is thrive

What does that mean
about who I am?
How do I define
the goals and the plan?

I'm good at standing in my own way
Even when I know better
The energy and momentum carries me
Until I'm way off center

So as I write this
At the breakfast table
I'm grateful for those
Who have been stable

I want to expand
I want to grow
Not die from a lost focus
that longs to show.

Clear the notifications
if you must
Our relationship
must've had to bust

There'll be others
Who will inspire
And maybe, just maybe
I won't have to be as tired

It makes me sad
Cause it's still a loss
a "what if" dream that's not as bad
a lesson that has to be flossed

Thank you for the time
that was so dear
before the extra stress
and before you had to hit clear

I'm moving on,
although I don't know where
See you around
and will fist bump you there

And hey, I'm writing poetry
something to cheer!

Dear Reader, now it's your turn to write. Use the space below. Don't censor yourself.

How have you found community helpful?

Stacy Belinsky is the Owner of Serendipity Spot, LLC, and an expert in helping women entrepreneurs experience the magic that unfolds through being in community with others through hosted events. Participants fill in knowledge gaps, gain friendships and new skills, and find stress relief related to business and in their lives. Stacy resides in West Michigan and finds JOY and FREEDOM riding her bicycle as much as possible in all seasons. Learn more about event offerings at http://stacyjbelinsky.com

Chapter 11

Love Letter to My Missing Soul Sister

Emily Atlantis Wolf

My Story

Dear Other Emily -

It's me, your sister. I just discovered why I'm here, the big mission - soul purpose. I was just talking to my dear friend, Sarah Sparks, who channels God for a living. Over Zoom. I'd be happy to introduce you.

She asked me, "Do you believe you're an infinite being?"

I paused and answered, "Yes."

No one had asked me that question before. That's why I paused. But yes, I believe I'm living a multitude of lifetimes (until I get off the karmic hamster wheel) as an eternal soul.

Then she asked, "Do you know your soul's purpose?"

I paused again and answered, "Yes."

This pause was me asking my Soul about my/our purpose. 'Gather women' was the answer I got. That was new to me. I thought I was here to help the Earth birth her next evolution. (With tons of other people. Obviously. But maybe gathering my sisters is how I can help.)

It slipped a cog into place in the wheel of my brain. Ahhhhh! That's why I have no living mother, no aunts, no grandmothers, or no blood sisters in my life. My soul set this up, so I'd need to gather women around me. My longing has a purpose. So, I'm gathering my tribe one sister at a time.

I'm looking for you, my missing soul sister. And I'm wondering what you're like. Are you out there in the world wondering if you're living the life you really want to live?

If you're like me, you're a seeker. You sense that there are many layers to living, and most of them have nothing to do with working in a cubicle, making polite conversation, or staying in unfulfilling relationships.

Or maybe, like me, you're doing all those things and wondering how to get out of them, out of the labyrinth. I can show you. I'll walk with you. It starts with curiosity about what's on the other side of living the way you are now. Then you do something to disrupt your life, like quitting your job and going to massage school. Never doubt you can choose a different life. And change only happens in a blink.

So, Other Em, I'm sending this message to you in the hopes that we can find each other and remember when we were sisters in the wild woods, sitting around an evening fire, drumming, singing, and finding our joy in shared stories and shared silence. I created so many ways to help us find each other—free Zoom coaching calls, breathwork events, and retreats.

And I wrote you four poems. If they spark an interest, come find me. I can teach you to write.

The first three poems are haikus. They have a 5-7-5 form. The fourth one is about sex majik. Have you heard of it? It's when a woman holds a request in her mind while she practices the act of self-love. It's a doozie. Quite a feat to pull it off. Hope you like it.

Love, Your Seeking Sister, -Emily Atlantis

The Poems

August in Shaker Heights

Wet. Sweat. Rivulets.
Sun. Fun. My bra hooks undone.
Shade. And lemonade.

Dragon Medicine Woman

Firekeeper. Shaman.
Curandera. Madre. Queen.
She is Emily.

After My First Shamanic Breathwork

My Mind's Minotaur –
Beware! Your labyrinth is
Now my Dragon's lair.

Lesson 27: How To Conjure Your King

Ladies, your body is a temple
And it's time to pray.

You're here in my world, created for you,
A place from my past, no windows, no view.

Sand floors for your blankets, shaded by stone
Walls that reach apex to muffle your moans.

Time to light Kyphi now that it's dusk,
Pass the blue lotus, wear it like musk.

My Egypt and I welcome you, Sisters,
Ready to conjure your majik Misters?

Start with your body. Rest on the floor.
Drop your clothes here. You've reached your far shore.

Breathe in the darkness, the horror and gore.
Call to your Lilith, your Crone, and your Whore.

Breathe out the chains and colonized bindings,
Unheard rage and low groans. Legs unwinding.

Breathe in the Mother,
Breathe out the Maiden.

Close your eyes, rest your hands, let your DNA stray.
Call back drumming, chanting, and howling wolves today.

You've done this before,
Reach back,
Reach back,
Reach back.
With sisters, in circles,
Before The Attack.

What do you want?
What do you crave?
What's your desire?
What opens your lips?
What frees your hips?
What feeds your fire?

Have it.
But follow the law:
Harm to none.
No one is flaw.

Today we pretend it's a man that we need.
Pick your pronoun, dear sisters. Now we proceed.

Breathe in the Mother,
Breathe out the Maiden.

1. Root
Start in the dark, like seeds in black soil.
Legs growing roots, Shakti quivers, "Uncoil!"

Call in Pacha Mama, your Dreamer, your Earth,
Your rock and your water, assembled before birth:

"Thank you, Madre Tierra, for this borrowed body.
I'm steward to this flesh, this temple, this poppy.

Bless my request I'm making today,
Humbled, surrendered. Please find a way.

Bring me my man, my lover, and king.
A sword and a shield, a strong back and wings

Arms that reach round, holding my shadow and light,
The wholeness of me, with all of his might.

A man who stands
As my protective tree,
A place to climb in,
A space to be me."

That is my wish, now make it your own.
Ladies, make a man who feels like a home.

Breathe in your Mother,
Breathe out your Maiden.

2. Womb
Now it's time to stir your cauldron: Hand and man,
Spark the fire and greet your Hooded Woman,

Yoni, the guardian to your Cave of Creation.
Part her folds, warm her walls with your breath of elation.

Slip your hand in your slit, stirring your pot.
The other hand wanders, finds her own spot.

Stirring in circles, slow cyclical waves,
Keeping King present. What would he say?

Find your rhythm, build your heat, one lick of flame.
It's a rise, not a race, a feminine game.

Breathe in your Mother,
Breathe out your Maiden.

Breathe in your Mother,
Breathe out your Maiden.

3. Plexus
Keep circling and spiraling, pull it up toward your chest,
A gradual build, a long spell 'til nest rest.

Tap into the infinite moment, Here and Now,
By saying, 'I am,' steeped in your power.

"I am God and Goddess, thunder and rain.
I am Divine Mother, blood in the vein.
I am Spirit and body, ocean and air.
I am Hathor and Mary, bone and hair.

I call in my equal, my partner and mate.
My companion, teacher, my worth-the-wait."

Breathe in your Mother,
Breathe out your Maiden.

4. Heart
Keep drumming and strumming, reaching your center,
Stroking and coaxing and feeding the embers.

Stride high into Soul's Chamber,
Altar of Heart.
Bring him, too;
You were never truly apart.

Here is the bridge where form kisses dream,
Wish conception, where wave crests gleam.

Time to swirl dust around your construction.
Dream big, my sisters, is my instruction.

See his hands, his shoulders, and his angelic face.
The holy gift given to you by the Three Fates.

Imagine your bodies entwined and united,
Your heartbeats joined in concert, divinely guided.

Breathe in your Mother,
Breathe out your Maiden.

5. Voice
Together as one, rise into your throat.
The others before him? Release with a smote.

Is this the moment he whispers your name?
And you, Enchantress, will you do the same?

Humming and toning, a bell ready to ring.
Groaning and moaning, a lynx ready to spring.
Ladies ablaze, living inferno, inhale. Sing:
"Bring me, bring me, bring me my King!"

Breathe in your Mother,
Breathe out your Maiden.

6. Eye
The final ebb before we all flow.
The pause after exhale. Easy. Slow.

Widen your view, see with one eye.
A galactic approach, a cosmic sky.

Imagine - yesterday -
You and he,
Sacred communion,
Knitted yourselves together,
Forever in union.

Imagine each day, and day, and day,
A lifetime together, an endless array.

What is different? What is same?

What will he teach you?
What will you learn?
What will be undone?
What will you burn?

Breathe in your Mother,
Breathe out your Maiden.

Breathe in your Mother,
Breathe out your Maiden.

7. Crown
Now Witches and Queens, it's ebb to flow,
Let your fires blaze brightly. Up to O!

Let go of tethers, anchors, and strings,
Grab yourself hard, feel all the zings.

Soften your gates. Let him in. Let him in.
Imagine his mouth where your hand is.

Dance like a dervish with your Hooded Woman.
Faster swirls and twirls. Heave your bosom.

Rise from your roots, hips to nips.
Give voice to your thunder, out your lips.

Let the lava seek the peak, unable to fall.
Crack open your flesh, release it all.

Blast through the rocks, the fissures and cracks,
Claim the Goddess now. She's back!

Wave after wave, pleasure unleashed.
Celestial flying. Chances increased.

"This or something better for my King and best friend.
I trust you, Divine Source. To the end of the end."

Breathe in your Mother,
Breathe out your Maiden.

Breathe in your Mother,
Breathe out your Maiden.

Breathe in your Mother,
Breathe out your Maiden.

And so it is.
Aho.

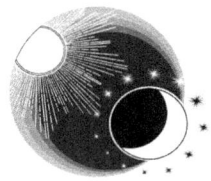

Dear reader, it's your turn to write. Use the space below. Don't censor yourself.

Use this space to write what you're afraid to say, whether it's too racy, erotic, vulnerable, or cheerless to say out loud. You may be surprised how good it feels to move emotions out of your body through your hand. Besides, you can always rip this page out of the book and burn it up, sending the energy back to the stars.

Emily Atlantis Wolf is a professional healer and guide. (That means she gets paid to invent unique ways to help people.) She climbed corporate ladders in civil engineering and financial services until 2009, when her mom died. She pivoted into the healing arts, becoming a Shaman, Master Breathwork Facilitator, and Licensed Medical Massage Therapist. Since 2010, she has helped over 3,000 clients confront and care for their physical and metaphysical pain. From chronic muscle tightness to trauma and unexpressed emotional energy, Atlantis combines practical and intuitive modalities. Part of her secret is connecting to spiritual realms using breathwork, drumming, fire ceremonies, and the guidance of galactic dragons. She holds group calls (free), online writing courses, breathwork events, and retreats. Sign up for her email list to receive a free video showing you how to release one piece of stuck energy with drumming and fire.

https://www.atlantiswolf.com/

Chapter 12

Nectar or Poison: Words Wound or Heal

By Lulu Trevena, Artist, Soulful Living Coach

My Story

"This way," ushered the bright, youthful waitress to the patio. The air was still sticky in late summer. The soft whirr of overhead fans assisted the relief of the heaviness in the air and my mood. My friend arrived within minutes, smiles and greetings exchanged.

She leant forward calmly, her eyes soft and safe, "Hey Lulu, what's up sweetie?" drawing each word out slowly, with care and concern. I've never had a good poker face; seems there was no hiding my weighty burden. I looked up briefly to meet her eyes and promptly looked down. My hands were clammy, and my heart drummed audibly, distracting my thoughts briefly. My throat ached, that dull, all-encompassing ache, and my jaw was tight.

I gingerly looked up, "Can I ask you something?"

"Yes, go ahead," attentively.

I swallowed, no ease forthcoming! My eyes were unsure where to rest.

"Has your husband ever called you a crazy bitch?" Her eyebrows pinched together.

I went on, all the words clambering to come out, and me dearly wanting them no longer rattling around in my consciousness.

"Has your husband, at any time, called you crazy, called you a bitch, called you a fucking crazy bitch?" Her face was ashen—cold, steely ash.

"No never," reaching her hands across the table towards mine.

I blurted out, "Did your first husband?"

She took my hands in hers. Again, calmly replying, "No, does yours?"

My face stung with pain; I squeaked out, "Yes."

"Did he apologize?"

I bowed my head, "No."

"Did you tell him that it is not okay to talk to you like that?"

"Yes, every time. I tell him it hurts me when he says that."

Every time hung heavy, in the café patio. We both noticed.

Her hands squeezed mine gently. Our eyes locked, mine blurry with tears.

"Lulu, you know that it's not okay that he says those things, don't you? It's demeaning. You know you do not deserve that! It's verbally and emotionally abusive."

The only thing holding me now was my seat, the table, and her hands; I felt like I was spinning. My stomach had a purging sensation, not what you want in a restaurant patio. I grabbed my water glass thirstily, then moved it to my forehead, offering to regulate my heat and light-headedness simultaneously.

With more directness, "Lulu, you don't deserve that, ever!"

Sometime later, I brought this pain to couple's therapy. The therapist was warm and supportive of me and very direct with my now ex-husband.

Words can truly harm. The old saying, *Sticks and stones can break my bones, but words will never hurt me* is absolute BS. Emotional and verbal abuse shows no visible scars, and the effect can be devastating. Ask a child who has been verbally taunted by classmates—scarring! Hurtful and demeaning words said to our loved ones, or anyone, can wound deeply. When done often, doubt arises, corroding self-esteem, even in the strongest of people. Words can be nectar or poison—in the classroom, office, sports field, or home.

We all have ingrained loops and patterns, often installed by others (psychology says this happens even preverbally and genetically—epigenetics). It's my dedication to myself that I recognize, uninstall, delete, and remove them. I hold my heart, mind, inner child, and soul sacredly. I've upgraded to tenderness. I feel blessed to have loving, affirming friendships. There is great importance to be witnessed lovingly in our dark times. Find your safe people. My own self-talk has become so deliciously tender, gentle in a cooing way, like I would do with a small babe. A loving ally.

The Poems

When you are careless

when you are careless
instead of caring
it injures

when you use sarcasm
instead of sincerity
it wounds

when you withhold or withdraw
instead of connect and embrace
the pain is unbearable

love thrives
with the ingredients of
care, sincerity, and connection

turning away with detachment
is in opposition
to running towards in partnership

Betrayal

betrayal
leaves a gaping wound

unmasked
revealing the deceit

grappling
with pain drenched questions

the confusion
was any of it true

a collection of memories
scattered haphazardly

broken shards
of empty commitments

shattering
trust and discarding intimacy

places
of secret anguish

wedding vows
laced with future war

the betrayal
a reflection of action
choices of the betrayer

not one
doubting value or worthiness
of the betrayed

tempting
to numb out the pain
society markets vices everywhere

do not succumb
to burying it inside
there it does not belong

purge
out the bitter shrapnel

exhaust
the tears flowing through your veins

remedy administered
by the love reclaimed within

rebuilding
the self-sovereignty that lapsed

erect the palatial walls
foundations strong

new boundaries
to guard the heart

discover the treasure
in all of who you are

sit upon
the throne of your wisdom

cloaked
in personal resurrection

warmed
by the illuminating fires of healing
held safely

watched over
by a divine host
of unseen guardians

no longer will betrayal sneak in
like a thief
wearing clothing you found familiar

theirs

or

your own

She Emerged

witness the part
that is dying
that held on too long
bargaining
and begging

she emerged
as if from another world although
she was never
not there

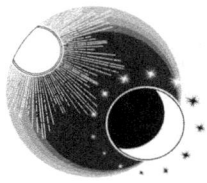

Dear Reader, now it's your turn to write! Use the space below. Don't censor yourself.

Nectar or Poison

Explore in your writing, words you have or would like to receive in the way of nectar; the sweet, luscious, delicious kind. Bonus: Start saying these to yourself. Explore words that have been like poison when you were a child and now. Opportunity: Afterward you might like to cross these poisonous words out.

Lulu Trevena is a multi-award-winning author, artist, women's workshop leader, mother, and Soulful Living Coach who's passionate about shifting the societal narrative about women and age.

Her stunning hardcover art and poetic prose book *"Soul Blessings,"* won the 2018 Silver Nautilus Book Award. Becoming a published author after 55. She is the creator of the card deck, *Moments of Transformation,* and journal, *Epiphany Journal and Playbook.* She is the founder of Live Life with Wonder. Lulu is the lead author of *Wholehearted Wonder Women 50 Plus* and a contributing author in many titles in the healing and wholeness genre.

Lulu is an avid world traveler; when at home, you can find one of her cats purring on her lap. She believes a new depth and breadth of personal tenderness is needed for ourselves. She inspires others to be awake to meaningful moments and the beauty within and all around us as a life practice.

https://livelifewithwonder.com/

Chapter 13

Ever Wish You Could Turn Back Time?

By Linda Aileen Miller, LMT, CD(DONA)

My Story

Meeting a friend for coffee and heading to sell some timeless treasures will be a double-edged sword. Difficult to part with material things? Yes, because they have meaning. They once defined me. No doubt, I will cry. Lord, I hope it's not snot-dripping crying.

What does safe look like to you? Can you measure it? Can you feel it in your bones?

Remembering the day I got my black-faced diamond-studded Rolex means something. Well, it meant something then. It meant we had managed to piss away enough money on a watch that sat in a safety deposit box for the better portion of thirty-three years—my status symbol in the '90s. I still feel attached to it. I have a two-toned stainless and gold, diamond-studded Rolex for at least a few more hours.

Whoop-t-phucken-dew!

I can't pay my electric bill. It's on 'Final Notice.' I'm grateful they'll accept half. So, I'll sell my Rolex, some family gold, and other vintage pieces. I'll be grateful and relieved by nightfall. I won't be flat broke, unable to pay my way; something I could always do. I'm grateful and relieved that my status symbol will carry me for a month or two.

From broke to surviving is a very short trip.

Feeling grateful and sad simultaneously. Closed my Safe Box and turned in the keys. Those treasures I kept safe for $100+ annually rarely left the 'box.' $100+ multiplied by thirty-three years amounts to $3,300+ safely tucked away. Now, they'll keep *me* safe, with at least what the box cost to keep *them* safe, so *they* could one day keep *me* safe. Who knew?

The Knower knew. My gut knew. The soul of my cells knew.

As I pull around my curved driveway, new tires bump over old oak roots. Being home feels lighter. Safe. Swollen red eyes stare back at me from the rearview mirror. Pausing to silently thank those who proudly wore their diamonds and gold a hundred-plus years ago, with one big breath, I thanked myself for knowing it was time to let them all go. "Good job, YOU!" I proclaimed out loud, "Good job."

The tears begin again, with just a tiny smile creeping in.

Things can never replace a genuine hug.

"They don't know you, Linda." The scowl on her beautiful face rips my heart like razor-sharp box cutters. My daughter-in-law repeated, "They don't know who you are. It's not personal!" as my grandsons cowered behind her. Tears grab my throat, swallowing the words, "Who chose to discount my existence? Who never invited me to a single holiday celebration?" Was my part not using my voice? No.

For decades, I've been entrusted to hold space for traumatized children. We sit in the muck together, wading patiently for the healing that ultimately comes. Myofascial Release escorts miracles when the stars align. Strangers know me, see me, trust me, hug me. It reminds me of the song from The Who's Tommy. "See me, Feel me, Touch me, Heal me."

"He feels like he has to choose between you and his dad," she said.

Divorce dives deep.

My grandsons are six and eight. We've never shared a Disney trip or a sleepover. Rarely do we share a hug. Sacred days of bonding are gone. Are those lost forever? "They don't know you, Linda!" is personal.

I'm their grandmother, their blood. The only mother their father has! I'm their grandmother! I'm one of two. Call it whatever you will—Nana, Mimi, Gram, Sassy, E-ni-ci—all the same, by any other name, is still Grandmother. That's personal. May you never feel the pain of not being a part of your family's family. It is very personal indeed.

The Poems

In 2007, I self-published my first book of prose, ponderings, musings, and meanderings in a simple format for my inner circle. They encouraged me to go bigger, and *Who Is That Woman?* expanded my lifelong love affair with writing, one of the most powerful healing tools I know. Having said that, sixteen years later, I offer you...

Who Was That Woman, Daddy?

Who Was That Woman, Daddy?
I
Wish
I had
Known...
No!
I
Wish
They had
Known
No!
I wish
my grandchildren
AND
I had known each other.
It seems I was the only one interested in being a priority,
OR
even a tiny dangling participle in their lives.
Guess the good birth parents slept through that part about Honor Your Father and Mother.
HONOR? HA!
I've settled for simply being an inkling inclusion.
I'm done with settling.

Never in eight years did we share a holiday on the holiday.
Not even Groundhog Day
Or
Juneteenth!
For the love of God…
And…No!
It's not my angry foul mouth!
I don't curse in front of my grandsons.
Of course, with twice-a-year two-day visitations, I certainly have cause to…
I'm leaving soon
For parts unknown
It may be the scariest thing I've ever done
This is
My last chapter.
Making it matter counts
Making it count matters
Far more when you can see
The finish line
Yep! It's exciting and bone-shakin' scary!
And…
In seventy-six years
I've done some pretty exciting
Pretty wowunderful
Pretty amazingly awesome
Pretty down-right supercalifragilisticexpealidoious scary stuff!
I wonder if one day my grandsons will ask…
"Who was that woman, Daddy?"

Purging six generations can turn up rustic rubble and timeless treasures. "Great Aunt Lil," on my father's mother's side, was one of my favorite ancestors. I've kept a box of her belongings, and among them were official government papers regarding her only son, Corporal Christopher K. Monahan, killed in Germany during WWII. Chris is buried in Norway. He received a double bronze star for his 'caring of others who were injured in the streets.' I found his papers and received a voicemail I thought was either a weird coincidence or a scam. I don't believe in coincidences; that left scam, or not! This woman takes family members on treks through Europe to the resting places of loved ones whose bodies were never returned to the USA. Strangers tend their gravestones. The grave tender for Chris reached out to this woman, Kaye, for a picture. He wanted a face to put with the name nearly eighty years after Christopher's death. Tracing our family through White Pages, she found me. Aunt Lil spoke of Chris in the hushed tones of a long-grieving mother. Saved in a box of his belongings, from childhood through teen years into military times, was his compass, returned by US Government officials in 1945. Then my hand fell softly onto the leather strap of his military issue "trench watch," which he was wearing when he died. I sobbed for a long time and still do. When Kaye received the pictures of him, she sobbed too. Researching him for years, seventy-eight years after his death, someone who never saw his face still cares that he lived.

After I'm Gone

FOR CHRISTOPHER

After I'm gone
Who will know
The life I led
The road I chose?
Will anyone care
Or give a flip?
Google my name
Or check the list?
Finding the grave
Of a 'cuz'…long gone
Has prompted me
To keep pushing on.

Reading the words
From WWII
His Bronze Star rescues
Keep pulling me through.
For most of my life
Only knew his name
Now, knowing him more
Is changing my game.
In his lifeless 'trench watch'
Among his Mother's treasures
I can feel
His *still* heart-beat
Gently holding it
As it gently holds me
Shaking
From head to feet.

Sacred time is all we have
When life is said and done.
Time and remembering
We truly are all ONE.
What we do every day
In plain sight or cloaked
Changes this world
Long after we croak!

I had a choice
A black-faced diamond-studded
Rolex
OR
A WWII Trench Watch…
From a man, I never knew
Which would you choose?

Dear Reader, now it's your turn to write. Use the space below. Don't censor yourself.

"Ever wish you could turn back time?" Is your prompt.

Let yourself use this page to share a time of making a tough decision and the outcome. No rules except one—just let go!

Linda Aileen Miller, LMT, CD(DONA), is a Reiki Master and expert Myofascial Release Therapist who loves facilitating safe space for others to heal. She has spent nearly a quarter of a century supporting those healing the effects of PTSD.

This Certified Birth Doula and fierce advocate for the unborn holds space for both birth and loss in life. She has studied for the past three years with Amy Wright Glenn, Founder of The Institute for the Study of Birth, Breath, and Death, and will complete her Holding Space for Loss Consultant Certification this Fall.

An eight-time published author/poet with two #1 Amazon Brave Healer Productions, Bestseller collaborations, and one Amazon #1 New Release of her own, *he/HIM/his the imposter was real.* Linda helps you embrace authentic healing filled with balance, love, peace, and beyond.

If you'd like to know more about Christopher's story and see pictures of him as a young child and a Bronze Star Soldier, reach out to Linda here:

https://theinnerjourneyproductions.com/

Linda@lovingbirthjourneys.com

Thank you for embracing the work I love and the words that shake your cells!

Chapter 14

Leaving Paris in Tears: Unlocking The Magic Within

Silfath Sophia Pinto, Wisdom Keeper, Somatic Artist, Spiritual Visionary

My Story

After the immigration check, my phone rang; it was my best friend.

"I am at the airport! Where are you?"

I felt a tightness in my heart and answered:

"I just passed immigration."

Silence. She responded:

"I came to say goodbye one more time."

We both stayed silent; it was too late. I heard the disappointment in her voice. We said goodbye on the phone. I was flooded by a rush of emotions, but I thought, *Silfath, a security check isn't the place for you to have a meltdown.*

I contained my tears. As I was walking towards the boarding area in the middle of this busy Charles De Gaulle airport, each step made me realize what I was leaving behind with my new life in New York. Each step felt heavier with each realization: my two best friends, my brother and my sister, my hairdresser (you know how hard it is to find the perfect hairdresser for you?!), breakfast at my favorite café, eight years in France—the list was adding up!

I was so excited preparing for my move to New York that I didn't take the time to face all I was leaving behind. Yes, it was a new chapter I was really excited about, but there was so much I was leaving behind.

I got to the plane and sat in my seat. I reached to grab my seatbelt, and there was no seatbelt! That was it; I melted and started crying. I couldn't stop my tears anymore. The steward came to me to check what was going on, and I complained to him, "The seat belt isn't working!" I made it sound like it was a catastrophe, and really it was—everything that was my safety blanket, my comfort zone—was gone! I cried myself to sleep.

Opening a new chapter often implies closing another one. And it can be painful. This new life I was so excited about in New York was also a new life without my family, my best friend, and my favorite hairdresser.

This was a great learning experience for me. I learned the polarity of joy and sadness, beginning and ending, and contraction and expansion. I learned the importance of saying proper goodbyes and ending cycles. I learned that grieving is an art and a necessary process.

I went through a couple of months of grieving. And I allowed it. Eventually, I emerged from my sadness and discovered theatre dance classes on Broadway. I stepped into my new life. This move to New York was a life-changing decision: I discovered somatic therapy and energy healing, I left a job in banking and started my own business, and I found myself, my soul purpose, and my voice.

Letting go is necessary for our evolution. Over the last 17 years of coaching and healing hundreds of people, I've seen many clients getting stuck because they haven't learned the wisdom and beauty of endings and/or they're afraid of letting go of people, places, and situations.

Here is the magic I uncovered: the more we trust our own evolution and the whispers in our hearts, the more we move through life with ease and uncover who we are and the magic within us. It's a game of evolution, possibilities, and inner power.

This is my invitation to you through the poems I share: dare to step into a new version of you, find beauty within each experience, turn broken pieces into a masterpiece, unlock your brilliance, and live your most ecstatic life.

The Poems

Turning Broken Pieces into a Masterpiece

We are remembering that we are
The universe in ecstatic motion

You see, my love
There is a light within you
That no one can shine on Earth
A unique radiance that your presence
Brings in the world
You are golden
Your essence is your light
Your presence is your sacred offering

You see, my dear
Your story is an epic odyssey
To unveil the Gold hidden within you
And become a Master Alchemist turning
Broken pieces into a masterpiece
Creating your very own Heaven on Earth

This light of yours shines brighter
As your spirit and your body merge
This Heaven on Earth starts with you
Coming home to your body
And remembering that this body is
Your sacred vessel in this epic odyssey
That life is

Yes, my love
Cutting through the maze of childhood traumas
Cultural conditioning and ancestral patterns
You are learning how to navigate
The universe within you
And be your own healer
In your body

It is time to remember
How to breathe through your tears
And ride the waves of your joy
It is time to remember
How to call your spirit back to your body
How to become ecstatic as you dance masterfully
And deliciously between darkness and light
Turning pain into gold, wounds into wonders

Yes, my dear
This is your invitation to walk your path now
To choose inner mastery and embrace
Wholeheartedly
Who you came here to be
What you came here to share
It is all encoded in every cell of your body

Please, please my love
Your light matters, your voice is needed
Let yourself shine brighter in the world
Do not take this invitation lightly
As you uncover and embody the gift you are
You create a ripple of love around you

Being Ghosted: A Return to Love

I think that's what they call being ghosted…
I sat on the bed, in shock and confusion
As the floor was collapsing beneath my feet
I was retracing the events of that day
So many questions
Yet, silence was the only answer

Truth is
I ignored the signs
I did
My body spoke to me but I did not want to listen
Because
I wanted us to work
I wanted our love story to last
So I ignored the red flags

He had hesitations at first
His commitment was inconsistent
He was NOT a full-hearted yes
Because he was still figuring out so much
About himself, life and his heart
He showed me in so many ways
That he wasn't ready
But I didn't want to see it

The thing is
I saw our "potential"
I wanted to believe in US
I held on to the moments

When he was sure
And downplayed the hesitations
I held on to the sweetness
We experienced together
And ignored the moments
Of confusion and illusions

After 3 days of shock
I decided to dive deep into my pain, my confusion
And face my childhood wound of abandonment
To heal my past and unveil more
Of the love within myself
And there it was
In the battlefield of my heart
My father wound
Him leaving when I was 7
That hole in my heart, a deep sense of loss
And the desperate impulse to fight
For a man to love me

The thing about your dad leaving
Is that you wonder constantly…
What did I do wrong?
Was I not enough?
Your self-worth takes a hit
And this relationship showed all of it to me, very clearly
I saw all the times when I accepted behaviors
That were beneath me
When I was NOT treated like a Queen
And my whole body knew I deserved better
But I felt the need to compromise
Because the little girl in me was trying everything
To avoid experiencing that abandonment
Again

As I was dancing in the dark chamber of my shadow
I had the most beautiful realization
The intensity of the pull I had towards this man
Was because our interaction awakened
My childhood wounds of abandonment
His inconsistency and half-heartedness
Were daggers planted in this old wound
Reviving a story I needed to release
He came into my life to help me see my invisible cage
His role was to help me heal my past
The stakes were high indeed
Not because he was my soulmate – as I thought
But because he was my entry point to restore my heart
And truly open to love, a love that is mutual and sacred

Finally I was done with this cycle of pain
Done falling in love with an illusion
Done deeming my light to cuddle his ego
No more looking at him blinded by the veil of my desires
No more loving him through the lenses of my fears
As I was freeing myself from this old wound
I was remembering a deeper truth
A wisdom I had doubted for too long
The deep yearning in my soul
And strong knowing in my heart
There it was
Love is the ultimate sacrament
Reverence is a foundation
Authentic relating is my way
My heart has always called for a royal feast
At the table of the Beloved
I wanted to feel drunk in the alchemy of deep love
Sacred connection and courageous unfolding

Sacred Lovers

This love
I have known, doubted, searched for, remembered
This love is sacred ground
For our wounds to heal
And our gifts to expand
For us to co-create a better tomorrow
He honors my worth
He basks in the magnetic field of my turned-on womb
He holds my shadow with unconditional love
I bow down to him with reverence and devotion
In awe of the masterpiece he is
His wounds and his fears, his brilliance and his gifts
We become medicine for each other
Remembering that kind of love
Was the price of being ghosted
And that was a magical remembering

Sacred Woman Manifesto

I am a manifestation of the Divine Feminine on Earth
I honor the sacredness of life, around me, within me
I am a sacred temple and I treat myself with honor and respect
I nourish my body, soul and mind with
Food, thoughts, words and actions that elevate me
My emotions are powerful messengers, all of them
I hold the space for them to be expressed and heard
As they guide me towards deeper alignment with my truth

I have deep reverence and love for Mother Nature
Listening to Her
Honoring Her
Dancing with Her
I feel her pulse in my womb
Her wilderness activates ancient knowing within me

I am a sensually sacred woman
I don't eat, I nourish
I don't walk, I sway
I don't wash my body, I worship my curves
I don't hold my tears, I let them run wild
My Feminine Radiance amplifies as I cultivate
My sacred turned on, tuned it and connected to my Body Temple
My warm presence and open heart heal others
I release stress, performance, attainment, judgment and victimhood
I slow down, breathe, nourish, indulge, feel
I take my pleasure and desires seriously

As a sacred awakened woman
I treasure Divine Sisterhood
My sisters reflect me, my fears, my brilliance
Each woman I meet and dance with is a beautiful mirror
Helping me identify shadows and heal
I am conscious of those gifts and grateful for my sisters
I see their beauty when they can't see it
I see their fears and shadows with tenderness
I welcome that every shadow, fear, gift and brilliance
Coming into our dance will be an opportunity for me
To realize, break free and blossom

I am a woman, I am medicine
I own the fire of creation and the infinite potential in my womb
I am life, I am love, I am a Creatrix
As I circle my hips, I create a powerful magnetic field
Breathing life into my body, into the Earth, into the world
Weaving sacred ceremonies and rituals into my life
I move with the divine, everyday
Howling on the New Moon
Drumming on the Full Moon
Sacred dance in the morning
Sage burning in the evening

I remember that I am wild and wise
I see beyond the visible, I hear beyond the audible
Anchored by my razor-sharp intuition
And powered by my extra sensory perception
I embrace the flow and mystery of life
I unveil the beauty in every moment
I turn pain into purpose, like a true artist
Painting a masterpiece with lost pieces
I surrender to the Infinite Intelligence of Life
And I dance with Her, gracefully, peacefully, authentically

Dear reader, now it's your turn to write. Use the space below. Don't censor yourself.

Take a deep breath. Close your eyes. Feel your heart.

And write: what my soul is really calling for now is…

Silfath Sophia Pinto is an Energy Alchemy Coach, a practitioner of the Healing Arts, and a Transformational Speaker.

Over the last 13 years, Silfath has supported leaders, change-makers, and organizations through her unique methodology, LuminEssence, a fusion of somatic therapy, subconscious reprogramming, and energy coaching. She has led 25 retreats and hundreds of experiences around the world, including Bali, Dubai, Cape Town, Greek Islands, Fiji Islands, New York, Lagos, and Abidjan.

Silfath's unique approach to raising our consciousness and reality creates deep shifts at a physical, emotional, mental, and spiritual level. Through this methodology, her clients harmonize their careers, family relationships, love life, finances, and health.

They call Silfath a soul whisperer, a happiness magician, and an angel of transformation.

Get your "Empowered and Ecstatic Embodiment" Starter Kit at

https://silfathpinto.com

Chapter 15

The Heart Knows

Dr. Pamela J. Pine

My Story

The Heart Knows

As we do sometimes, for years, against all the odds, in addition to the peaceful years, we may try to be a part of another's life.

I told you early, "What a breath of creativity and fresh air you are in my work and life."

But that atmosphere changed soon, too, didn't it? I wrote to you in an attempt to understand, "You needed to save face, be the center of it all (I now understand the need). First was the denigration of me, and now the clandestine messages, songs, movie clips, FB re-orientations, hacking, reels, all of this, while we both try to reach each other and stay connected in very, very different ways."

After two years of clandestine and direct attacks, with others believing and repeating your lies of things I did not say or do, I paced up and down my long driveway, on the phone to my far-away brother-in-law in California, making high-pitched screeches and mumbled, terrified, "What do I do, what do I *do*?" That was the closest I've ever gotten to wondering if I'd wind up in a psychiatric hospital.

After seven years (I always knew that was a special number) of cowering, fear, annoyance, anger, and sometimes fury at the lack of willingness to take my desires and requests into consideration, at the underhandedness, manipulation, malignment, and cruelty, I sputtered this:

"You think I should have further compassion and empathy, to have a desire to walk any further in your shoes - to try to feel anything that you feel or understand any more than I have tried to for way too many years only to get my lamb brought to the slaughter over and over again, or embrace the symbolic image you sent of a delicate flower emerging from the ice cold earth symbolizing this 'relationship,' or to ever work with you again, you lying, manipulative, destructive, mean, cruel, underhanded asshole?

"Never have I ever felt the need to write to anyone in this 'tone of voice.' We all have reasons—ultimately, it's how we handle them and what we do with them that make us who we are.

"You have lost the game—and the best fucking friend you had along with it.

"But you needed to crush me into the ground repeatedly. You think I don't understand it? I do. It sucks. Get help."

If honesty is to prevail, the attention you showed me in our "relationship" was more at certain times than others, flattering and endearing. You mirrored me and said just the right words when I was down. "Look at all you've done," you said when no one seemed to really appreciate that effort. I felt seen, revered. I kept hoping for the right connection, whatever that connection would look and feel like, and wherever it would lead.

I read to understand you. I wrote to connect, share, and mend. I continued to invite you in. I left my heart open. I was also engulfed, confused, troubled, disoriented, disturbed, oppressed, traumatized, and enraged.

Finally, I realized (my heart told me): *If connection is to move forward, it needs to change; it needs to serve all those in it.*

I hit a holding wall. Holding walls hold up the house. They're critical to the integrity of the structure.

One needs to be careful what machinery one allows to be used against that wall—even if it's for renovation purposes.

I tried. I really tried. Connection is important, after all.

But the heart comes to decide. The heart knows. And it speaks. All we need to do is listen.

The Poems

Take Me to The Someplace Else

The brightest stars in that night sky detailed Orion
Who regained his sight after being blinded,
Delivered not only from the dark
But into the full color of days

Take me to that someplace else,
Beside the boulders that surround the sea
Where wildflowers grow around the stones
And golden pollen is released on a breeze,
Where the presence is as solid
As free

Direct my steps to that place,
Where I can sit when I am tired
While I smell the fragrances in the wind
Where I can walk beside you
With my feet in the sand
Where cold water laps
Leading us
Toward a fire
Waiting to be

It's so much work
To keep the color at bay
To erase the blues of a Caribbean ocean,
To ignore the warmth and wonder of a tropical son.
Why would I try –
But to punish the gods –
Rather than celebrate
Starlight from the Heavens

Rising from the Slaughter

Peaceful resolution
From a "soldier of truth"?
Hah!
A few inanimate words
Was all it took
To unsheathe your sword
And aim your terms
But then afraid
Of a backlash (on you)
You called a live "truce"
(Of a false kind)
By the time
I lay torn and tattered
By you and your wolves
Given what you'd fed them.

So, this is how it ends,
With a whimper meant to kill
It is years since. . .
We fell,
Since your sword first cut
Since your lies tore into gut
Since you've witnessed
What you should not
And now the door
That was cracked open
Through which for you to peep
For so long
Is broken

While other gates unlatched
On core wounds
Mine: not to harm
Yours: to get back
Lies and humiliation your tools
Of slaughter
Ours an explosive combination
While you insist
Your true interests
Are to understand,
To protect
But you knew. . .
You said:
"After what I've done. . .
Have some self-respect,"
while you continued to inspect
Yet now claim no clue
What you did, what you do
How could you not know?
You of all people should know. . .
And you do

I asked,
Nearly pleaded,
I will listen, I said,
I will try to understand.
I knew, though you pronounced it
There was never to be
Once upon a time
Not for me
Or for you
Instead, for at least a moment
"Never, ever" was your false, defensive call,
Just to stall
Bringing
No reconciliation
No resolution
No understanding
And so, I was forced not to face you,
But to flee you
In a crawl

Now again you want me to open,
You want me to trust, to share?
So again, "we" can rise?
But from what?
From ashes
Like the phoenix?
To what?
For what?
Your call for you
As you ascend from a nest of your lies
Delivering more crushing surprise
For me
I just rise,
With my sassiness
Diamonds
And rust

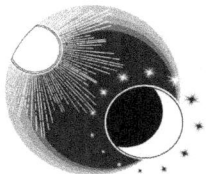

Dear Reader, now it's your turn to write. Use the space below. Don't censor yourself.

The heart comes to decide. The heart knows. And it speaks. All we need to do is listen. And grow. What is yours telling you?

Pamela J. Pine has been an international health, development, and communication professional throughout her adult life, concentrating on enhancing the lives of the poor and otherwise underserved groups throughout the world, with a primary focus on the prevention, treatment, and mitigation of child sexual abuse (CSA) and adverse childhood experiences (ACEs) for the past nearly 25 years. She was the Founder and former CEO of Stop the Silence˚: Stop Child Sexual Abuse, Inc. and, when Stop the Silence˚ became a Department of the Institute on Violence, Abuse and Trauma (IVAT) in January 2021, she became its Director. Additionally, she is a public health professor. She has also been a multi-media artist throughout her life, working in oils, watercolor, clay, song, and the written word (she is a published, best-selling author), which she also uses in her work to raise awareness and open hearts and minds toward action. Please see: https://www.drpamelajpine.com.

Chapter 16

Out of a Black Hole into the Light

DebS, Energy Release Facilitator

My Story

Go on, drive over the edge! Go on, drive off!
No one cares; nobody loves you!

I was driving across the Brecon Beacons when this suicidal voice urging me to end my life jumped into my head.

The marriage I thought was forever had ended. I felt hopeless, and my future seemed bleak. Those words shook me to my core.

I'd better see a doctor because I really need help!

At the doctor's, I broke down, sobbing, "I just need the details of a self-help group to get through this."

"And what about the depression?" she asked.

"I'm not depressed, just going through a bad patch."

Talk about being in denial! My doctor helped me realize that I'd fallen into a deep, dark, black hole of depression.

I was in a void, functioning on automatic pilot, but I believe that void, negative and dark though it was, gave space for the words to flow.

"Mum, I've written you and Dad a poem, it's called 'I Don't Understand But Thank You Anyway'. I don't know where it came from, but here, read it."

We cried, and my tears were finally tears of release. I managed to put into words what an abject failure I felt and how I couldn't believe that they still loved me anyway. It described the depths of my despair in ways I couldn't voice.

After this first poem, words flowed from pen to paper as if they were bypassing my brain and coming straight out of my hand. My pen became a wand, magically releasing some of the depth of my grief and utter desperation, and started to ease my pain.

"Why don't you get yourself a dog?"

"How can I look after a dog if I can't even look after myself?"

"It will give you something else to think about other than just you all the time. It will get you out of the house into the fresh air. You've become far too self-centered lately."

Direct words from my Mum sowed a seed.

Pip, my rescue dog, became my rescuer, and as my poems continued to flow, I grew stronger and happier. I retrained as a therapist and began to discover a newfound love and joy in life. Receiving unconditional love and experiencing joy began to fill the void with love and light.

Exploring new energy therapies, I had more realizations of connections with earlier times in life, past lives, and many more releases.

Oh my god, I've felt all these feelings before!

Damn, I've got a lot of work to do. How on Earth can I help other people if I've only touched the surface of my own stuff?

I took time out to reflect, release, learn, review, be thankful, and rejoice about my life. I learned to appreciate the darkness and the light, to rejoice in still being here.

This was mirrored in my poems—no longer all about me but about anything, and more importantly, now written with love.

The Poems

As you can see from my story, these poems connect with various stages of my recovery from depression. When I wrote this story and these poems, I had another spark of realization: they also connect with the various stages of healing that many of my clients experience during our sessions together. You may resonate with some, all, or none of it, but please reach out to someone to hold your hand, to hold space, and to help you through whatever your journey is. My wish is that you find your love and light and can rejoice in this particular precious life we have.

Realization

I fell into a black hole,
a deep void of despair
when there were days when I couldn't even get out of bed,
let alone put a brush through my hair.

But when did that dark hole appear?
Was it at the tender age of six
when my lovely Mum got taken away
and our family was left in a fix?

Or did it appear in my very first life
When I was a reptilian with a beautiful tail
And my sister and her friends attacked me
When she allowed her jealousy to prevail?

And my colourful tail - my identity
Was chopped off with terrible scars left
Outcast from the tribe with nowhere to go
Rejected, abandoned, bereft!

Did the hole appear in that moment
And each life's trauma increase its size?
Until this time I just couldn't take any more
And ending it seemed like a glittering prize.

But I didn't drive off that mountain
Something made me stay on the road
Was it an angel or an inherent survival instinct?
Whatever it was, it was in automatic mode.

But what I do know for an absolute fact
Is that a light bulb lit up and came on
The realisation that I needed to get help
For some reason I wasn't yet ready to be gone.

Release

Let your pen fly and glide over the page
Allow feelings to come forth, to escape from their cage.
Give your worries freedom from the cells in your brain
Allow solutions, not sorrows to be foremost again.
Investigate; explore; let that nib flow
Empty out those worries before they take hold and grow.
A light bulb moment might well occur
You may find links and connections where worries once were.
Look back and re-read all the words you have written
Is there a theme? For example: "twice shy, once bitten"?
Pull together significance, give it order and shape
Perhaps there's a story or poem waiting to escape?
There might be a lesson to learn of some kind
To improve an area of your body, soul or mind
Those words were imprisoned under lock and key
So let your pen loose and set all worries free.

Rescue & Recovery

Rescue dogs are heaven-sent; yes they're sent from heaven above
To rescue us poor humans and to shower us with love.

I certainly know that mine was my very own superhero
She came into my life and lifted me up from well below zero.

I'd decided upon her brother, but went back for one last look
She sauntered to the front of the pen and started a new chapter in my book.

She became my constant companion, my saviour, my sounding board;
My comedian and fitness guru; with her I could never be bored.

She filled my life and mended my heart, uplifted me when I was down
Made me laugh when she chased her tail and acted like a clown.

She watched me learn kinesiology moves, whilst walking in the rain
And allowed me to practice on her, when her body experienced pain.

She sat and watched while I 'tapped', to gave no clue what she thought
And when I sat to write my words, a comforting presence she brought.

She accepted my new partner and dogs they really know
If he'd have been a 'bad one'; I'm sure her teeth would show.

She left me when I was happy and content; she knew that I could cope
That my man was by my side and that my heart was full of hope.

Her furry body is no longer here, but the memories linger on
Her photo is on my windowsill and the joy will never be gone.

Dogs love unconditionally but I think rescue dogs give us more
Because on some level they understand that you rescued them, for sure!

So they want to show you gratitude and lick you from head to toe
To be your forever friend and to protect you from all kinds of foe.

But I want you to think deeply about who is really rescuing who
Because rescue dogs are heaven-sent and there's a reason yours chose you!!

Rejoice

What if I had actually done it?
Performed and executed that thought
Think of all the things I would have missed
And all the grief, my end would have brought.

I would never have learned the sheer love
Between a human being and her dog
I'd never have explored holistically
And released myself from my fog.

No more time to just sit and ponder
Nor meditate in the peace and the quiet
Bend and stretch my body in yoga
Or wonder whether I should go on a diet.

I wouldn't have broken an arrow with my neck
Nor walked over extremely hot coals
Listened to amazing live music
Nor achieved a single one of my goals.

I wouldn't have had any more fun
Or know what pottery clay's like to hold
Or laughed when it fell off the wheel
Or known what it would be like to get old.

I would never have found my rock
Who has stood beside me while I grew
Or realized that everything is energy
Despite a feeling that I already knew!

I would never have performed on a stage
Or even believed, that I ever could
I would never have become a tree-hugger
Each time I walked through the wood.

I wouldn't have met my nephews and niece
Felt their soft downy heads with my finger
Or seen them grow up over the years
Because I decided to no longer linger.

I would never have been able to travel
Or to have made so many new friends
Nor recognized my own programming
And understood all my life trends.

I could moan about the weather no more
Or watch starlings murmur in the sky
Be fascinated by all aspects of nature
Or to complain about time flying by.

I wouldn't have seen our planet
And its people be knocked off their feet
To be reminded to be grateful for all that I have
and learn to dance to a different beat.

I would no longer see the sun rise or set
Or gaze in awe at the silvery moon
Or guess shapes in the clouds as they floated by
Because I would have been gone too soon.

I would never have written any poems
Or discovered that I do have a voice
Or realized that our journey has a start and an end
But in between, that we all have a choice.

I used many energy therapy skills
To release and then finally let go
Of my deepest darkest beliefs and fears
To allow myself to live life in full flow.

I suppose my recovery truly began
The second I chose to stay on the road
An awakening seemed to occur within
Though it appeared to be written in code.

I wouldn't have had this enforced chance
To wonder what living really means
To look at my reflection in the mirror
And decide I must follow my dreams.

Writing this poem was a privilege
To show how gratitude can overcome fear
And because that day I did **NOT** kill myself
I can rejoice because I am still here.

Dear Reader, it's your turn to write! Fill in the blank(s). Don't censor yourself.

Having read 'Rejoice' which includes some of the things that make me glad I'm still here, write down all the things you have to rejoice about, no matter how big or small, how recent or long ago; continue it whenever something springs to mind and carry it with you as a reminder of how precious and wonderful life is.

DebS gains huge satisfaction from sharing her knowledge and self-help methods gathered over the past 30 years. In addition to writing poems, she does things that bring her joy. To keep her spirits up, she loves singing, dancing, and being outdoors, and to keep her body happy, she attends yoga classes and goes walking and cycling.

She wrote and self-published her memoir: 'The Day I Didn't Kill Myself,' with the goal of helping others going through divorce or depression to realize that there is life after this difficult and heartbreaking time.

She would love to empower you to discover your own SuperSonicSelf, so please reach out. Her powerful facilitation sessions involve the Helix Method, Akashic Records, energy kinesiology, and many techniques that helped her through her own darkest times. She works from the premise of: "I rise; you rise; we rise together!"

To connect with DebS: supersonicself1@gmail.com
https://www.supersonicself.com

Chapter 17

Burning Bright: A Poetic Journey of Self-Rediscovery

Nuria Gabitova, Edupreneur

My Story

If you were standing at an inevitable crossroads, surrounded by a pitch-black void of choices, yearning for the light to illuminate your decision, knowing there's no turning back, what would you do?

It's a moment that tugs at your very core, an important turning point, a fork in the road that demands a decision.

You feel the pressure building inside you, like a volcano about to erupt, bursting at the seams. Common knowledge whispers in your ear that there's no turning back, and you're faced with a choice that could change everything. You're caught between the agony of staying put, where the pain is known, and the allure of the unknown, where growth and transformation call.

Inside and out, you feel the pain. It's a visceral ache, a tightening of the chest, and a knot in the pit of your stomach. You're on the verge of a journey, one that promises to test your limits, challenge your beliefs, and shatter your comfort zone. It can come out as a disease, but no pills or doctor can fix it. The agony is real, hidden beneath layers of fear and doubt.

To go through, to truly transform, you must trust yourself. No one else can feel the pain of your growth for you. It's a journey you must traverse yourself. You can't skip the pain; you must embrace it—learn from it. You must look straight into the eyes of your own soul with an intensity that pierces the darkness.

Amid this emotional hurricane, there comes a moment of calm—a metaphorical eye of the storm.

Here, in the turbulence of self-awareness, change, and the rawness of pain, you pause. With profound listening, keen observation, and deep feeling, your mind and body merge into one. In the surrender state, you discover a healing you never knew existed. Instead of doing, you embrace being. You breathe and meticulously scan your inner landscape, granting yourself permission to experience every sensation, every emotion, fully and unreservedly.

One breath at a time. You breathe through the pain until you know the answer. It's there, deep within your gut, a knowing that transcends words. You trust your instincts, your breath, and your inner wisdom as you navigate this unknown path. Knowing you have wisdom beyond your conscious awareness, you melt into the energy of your own intelligence. Suddenly, you feel weightless, free, and clear.

I recently found myself in that process once again. Emerging from the cocoon of self-discovery, I felt like a butterfly, calm and strong. I know that my transformation has the power to create hurricane-strength waves, setting off a chain reaction of growth and healing in others.

When you find your purpose, the path illuminates before you, and the fear of the unknown crumbles away.

No one can do it for you, but you don't have to go through this journey alone. I realized at the end of my transformation that by learning how to be smarter with our feelings, building relationships with ourselves and others, and showing love and empathy to ourselves and others, we can continuously thrive and grow, even in the toughest times of uncertainty, without burning our wings or exhausting ourselves.

On my fork in the road, I chose to help young people learn skills that go beyond academic knowledge, skills that will empower them to embrace the pain of growth with resilience, intelligence, and grace.

Ready to embark on the poetic journey of self-rediscovery?

The Poems

Self awareness: Cozy Slippers for Your Soul

In the heart's serene depths so wide,
Imagine a cabin by the snowy forest's side.
The air so crisp, the world dressed in white,
This cabin's your soul's haven, snug day and night.

Cozy slippers adorn your feet just right,
As you bask by the fire, its warm, gentle light.
Your thoughts like flames, in the hearth they ignite,
Some gleam with hope, some dim in the night.

Guided by your mind's clear mirror, you gain the insight,
Each thought's origin and its soul-stirring flight.
A storm outside mirrors the turmoil inside,
Emotions swirl like winds, your soul as their guide.

Your self-awareness, a lantern, shining so bright,
Unveils self-judgment in the soft, glowing light.
You see your triggers, knots once tied so tight,
Instead of condemnation, you grant yourself flight.

In your soul's cozy cabin, free from the fight,
You shed labels like "*good*" or "*bad*," what a sight.
Accepting life's messiness, oh, what a delight,
Self-acceptance and self-love unite, shining bright.

Embracing your flaws, like stars in the night,
You see they're shared by all, a beautiful sight.
Kindness over judgment, a compassionate guide,
Building bonds of trust, relationships take flight.

Wonder why this skill wasn't taught? It's all right,
In a world chasing knowledge, inner wisdom took flight.
Now you stand at the door, your heart is so light,
Ready to embark on your journey, pure and bright.

With trust in yourself and the universe's might,
You're a beacon of light, dispelling the night.
As you navigate self, where clarity grew,
Master awareness, let your soul's brilliance debut.

With each breath, your soul's mirror comes in view,
Reveal your inner sun's light, a path to renew.
In the rhythm of your breath, self-awareness grew,
Transformation whispers softly, as the mirror reflects *you*.

Breathe In Awareness, Breathe Out Growth

Inhale, exhale—wait,
No fireworks, just air's embrace,
Breathing's same old fate.

Annoyingly plain,
No thrill, no cosmic insight gained,
Just air in and out.

But then I decide,
Let's turn this into a ride,
Belly inflates wide.

Like babies and animals, we start,
Full belly, then empty heart,
Breathing's a playful art.

Inhale like the breeze,
Exhale like wind through tall trees,
Life flows as we breathe.

Belly swells with air,
Then empties to spine with care,
Game of breath, so fair.

Breath, life's gentle force,
Awareness blooms, music flows,
Prana's dance, life's course.

Light as a feather,
Floating through any weather,
Me, myself, together.

No judgment, just peace,
Soul's mirror, clarity's ease,
Breathing, life's masterpiece.

Control, effortless grace,
In storms or tranquil embrace,
Breath reveals its space.

Weightless, aware, like
ninja, dodging triggers' storm.
Breath - strong currents transform.

Inhale courage, exhale fear,
Life's twists and turns, crystal clear,
Breath's wisdom, always near.

What I thought I knew,
Breath unveils life's grand debut,
Shining bright, I'm true.

Now I know the way,
Inhale, exhale - full on, seize the day,
With each breath, I play.

Dear reader, now it's your turn to write. Use the space below. Don't censor yourself.

Opportunity to Hone Your Emotional Ninja Abilities

Recall a recent trigger when you regretted your response. What could be the impact of pausing for one to three deep, mindful breaths before responding? Will you consider trying this next time you're triggered?

Congratulations on your small win, a step toward your emotional and mental fitness through mindful breath. One step closer to transformation!

Nuria Gabitova: Mom, Author, Edupreneur, and Compassionate Innovator™. She believes in the power of education to unlock the inner genius in every child by fostering emotional agility and mental fitness. Her mission is to empower young minds, their parents, and educators to shine!

Self-awareness is the foundation for emotional agility and mental fitness. You can discover your foundation strength and get personalized growth tips at: www.ischoolforthefuture.org/quiz

Chapter 18

Seasons Change: All is Fair in Love and War

Tanya Stokes

My Story

In the grand theater of life, we all have our seasons, those mystifying chapters woven into our existence. They emerge with a purpose, either to enrich our spirits or to fill an echoing void. But how do you interpret the season of another soul in your narrative? It's a dance of perception, a symphony of words, and a willingness to heed their whispers. For some, it's a web of challenges, while others read the script on the wall with a knowing smile.

Let me draw you into the captivating tale of *My Muse*, a chapter that unfolded with a request to the heavens, a plea for a Boaz to grace my path. And oh, what a moment it was when he knocked on my door! Imagine a vision of masculinity, standing tall at six-foot-four, dipped in chocolate, with shoulders broad enough to carry the weight of dreams. His smile, a beacon of allure, had the power to ignite passions. His words flowed with kindness, painting a portrait of action, openness, and transparency. There was humility in his essence, a rare gem in the realm of romance.

Our initial encounter was a whirlwind, a tempest of emotions that left me stumbling over my own heart. From the physical chemistry that could set the world ablaze to intellectual dialogues that ventured into realms of finance, future plans, and dreams, our connection was a tapestry of shared aspirations. I approached this chapter determined to break free from the shackles of my old-school thinking, forged in the fires of a failed 13-year marriage and a six-year-long rebound.

Yet, there's a twist in every story. I chose to ignore the red flags. The warning signs manifested in various ways, such as the absence of those small, intimate moments like his drive-by hellos during his workday that once defined the connection we once had. I also noticed a gradual withdrawal from our shared friend circle, as if he was deliberately distancing himself. Our daily conversations became restricted, and he even started putting his phone on "do not disturb" mode at night, creating a barrier to our communication. What troubled me most was his reluctance to take the initiative in our relationship. He seemed resistant to lending a helping hand without me having to ask, which left me questioning the depth of his commitment and our future together. But amidst the cracks in the facade, my spirit soared to new heights, my business flourished, and my confidence reached unparalleled peaks.

Then came the moment that shattered my world—a revelation on social media, a picture-perfect facade suddenly torn apart by the presence of another woman who shared my man. It felt like a sledgehammer striking my heart, breaking it into a thousand fragments right before my eyes.

A war commenced within my mind, body, and soul, not of swords and shields. Doubt and what-ifs took center stage, a relentless playback of every conversation, text message, and phone call. As my world crumbled, my mental landscape plunged into a dark abyss. Inner thoughts swirled with chaos, a relentless storm of self-doubt and despair. "How could this happen? What did I miss?" I questioned myself, feeling the weight of my inadequacy pressing down on me. "I thought we had something special, something real," I dismissed, memories of happier times haunting my thoughts. "Am I not attractive enough? Did I fail to keep his interest?" Insecurity plagues at my core, making me doubt every aspect of myself.

"I need to fix this, salvage what's left of us," I resolved, determination rising amidst the turmoil. But beneath it all, a profound sense of loss and betrayal cast a long shadow over my heart, and the road ahead seemed uncertain.

But from the ashes of despair, the phoenix of self-healing arose. Allow me to share how I'm embarking on the journey back to rediscovering myself:

1. Self-care, exercise, meditation, and the magic of books: To find my way back, I've embraced self-care as a daily ritual.
2. Affirmations and the echo of positivity: Affirmations have become my daily anthem, a chorus of positivity I sing to my reflection. I've created a list of affirmations that resonate with my spirit, recorded them, and put them on repeat. It's a constant reminder that I'm in control of my destiny, and my thoughts are the architects of my reality.
3. Sleep: I've learned to honor the sacred sanctuary of sleep. Without it, the balance of my thoughts teeters on the precipice. Sleep is not merely rest; it's the reset button for my mind, an essential ingredient in maintaining my inner equilibrium.
4. Nourishing the body, feeding the spirit: Eating has become more than a necessity; it's a form of self-love. Nourishing myself with wholesome food not only fuels my body but also provides the strength to face life's challenges head-on. It's a reminder that I deserve the best, both physically and emotionally.

In these four pillars of self-renewal, I'm finding my way back to the essence of who I am, piecing together the fragments of my being and emerging stronger, wiser, and more resilient than ever before.

The Poems

Writing has been my trusted companion on this journey, a form of therapy that has allowed me to navigate the depths of my soul and scale new heights of self-awareness. It's a brave endeavor to explore the recesses of one's own heart and mind, and it's through these words that I've uncovered hidden truths about myself. I hope you enjoy!

Be Brave

Your life's journey, an epic tale we've seen,
A transformation and resilience, the ultimate themes.
From marriage's heights to divorce's divide,
From two-parent bliss to single-parent stride.

In this intricate dance, between victory and fall,
You're a warrior, standing tall through it all.
Storms you've weathered, in hunger you've shared,
Through broken-down cars, you never despaired.

Two jobs you held, as a renter you knew,
Paying someone's mortgage, yet your spirit stayed true.
But your bravery, a guiding star's light,
Led you to homeownership, soaring to new heights.

Driving a car, debt-free, with pride you now steer,
A remarkable journey, so crystal clear.
In my eyes, you're not just winning the race,
You're a champion, an inspiration, full of grace.

Your children, contributors, to your community they've grown,
A testament to the love and dedication you've shown.Now, pursuing
dreams with an unyielding desire,
Your determination sets hearts and souls on fire.

So, remember, my friend, in this tale so grand,
Be brave, let courage guide you hand in hand.
Don't let others sway your chosen way,
You possess everything you need, every single day.

Your journey's a beacon, a courageous display,
Inspiring others as they find their own way.
Keep being brave, for yourself and for all,
A testament to strength, standing tall after each fall.

Step it Up

Get it, girl!
Make it happen,
Bring those dreams to life right now.
Don't let society's limits hold you back,
You're a queen,
Yes, I said it, QUEEN.

Be yourself, do what sets your soul on fire,
There are no boundaries to what you can aspire.
Seize that opportunity,
Sign that contract,
Take that role,
Step it up, take control!

You've got this, even when doubt creeps in,
Step on it and let your journey begin.
Escape the confines of your mind, my queen,
The world's your oyster, your stage, your scene.

You're the author of your story,
With the power to claim your glory.
With passion and truth, I say this to you,
And remember, I'm saying it to me too,
Step it up, embrace your inner hue,
You're unstoppable, boo!

Forgiving Healing

To forgive is to heal,
But mere words won't suffice; we must truly feel.

Feel the emotions, let them ebb and flow,
Allow them to pass through, and let their lessons show.

Learn to master them, to hold the reins,
Control your thoughts, and release your mental chains.

Reject insecurity and doubt's cruel game,
They're unwelcome guests, they're not your aim.

They are thoughts, not solutions to pursue,
For a better you, let healing renew.

Forgiving, healing, it knows no set time,
No calendar can measure this climb.

Healing follows its own path, undeterred,
Respect its journey, let it be heard.

The moment you do, your true journey begins,
Towards forgiving, and healing, where your soul wins.

Forgiving, healing, embrace their grace,
In their boundless journey, find your own space.

Journey

Indeed, healing is a journey, no rushing allowed,
It takes its own time, like a serene cloud.
No shortcuts to completion, it's a path we must tread,
Unresolved past traumas may haunt us instead.

Insecurities, heavy burdens we bear,
From fears of not being enough to those we're aware.
Fear of being too much, fear of words left unsaid,
In the bedroom or elsewhere, they linger like dread.

Some rush to relationships, it's all they've ever known,
But it's crucial to see, that healing is where strength is sown.
A relationship should complement, not a refuge be,
From the turmoil within, where our hearts long to be free.

Take the time to heal, a self-love so profound,
A commitment to self, in the heart, it's found.
Be whole and be healed, from the past's heavy chain,
Then in a new love, your true self will reign

Dear reader, it's your turn to write. Use the space below. Don't censor yourself.

I feel your pain. There is a reason for every season. It doesn't take away from who you are or whom you belong to. I want you to write what comes to your mind. Really get into it, lay everything out on the table! Okay, here you go, you've got this!

Write a thank you letter to your ex.

Tanya Stokes found her true passion in the world of graphic design. Specializing in bringing her clients' dreams to life, she excels in crafting logos, designing business cards, and creating striking book covers and websites. In 2018, she took a bold step forward, founding Compassionate Design LLC. The choice of the company name, "Compassionate Design," reflects her unwavering commitment to delving deep into her clients' vision, understanding their needs on a profound level, and creating designs that truly resonate.

For a closer look at her work, visit her website at: https://compassionate-designs.com/

Chapter 19

Align with Your Inner Truth

Ashley C. Hall, RYT-500

My Story

On a blazing August day, as my sister and I were hiking through Canyonlands National Park, I confided to her, "I'm only going back to school because I literally don't know what else to do."

"Don't go," she fired back. That hit me like a punch in the gut. *Don't go,* I thought, *what choice do I have?* I felt the discomfort of her words stirring something within me. I wanted to stuff that idea back inside, but I couldn't un-hear it.

"What do you really want to do?"

"I want to teach yoga."

This opened the floodgates to dive into my passions, a whole new world of dreams and possibilities. My inner wanderlust burst from within me. My inspiration, creativity, and life force energy moved through me like a rushing river. The vision of quitting my job, solo traveling to Costa Rica, and becoming a yoga teacher felt like painting rainbows across a gray sky. It was time to listen to the deep calling of my soul.

As I sat in the small coffee shop on South Broadway late one evening, I felt a surge of energy; I'd never wanted anything more in my life. *This is it*, I thought, as I clicked, 'book flight.'

I felt a bit lightheaded after riding the elevator up to the 39th floor. The view out the corner boardroom was breathtaking—a spectacular panoramic view of the Rocky Mountains. As I arrived at the ripe time of 7:45 a.m., I felt like a ghost floating through an empty house. It was a chore to drag my body to the office filled with suits.

I felt a contraction inside me. *You don't belong here. You belong somewhere that all of you is welcome, where your spirit feels free.* I wasn't utilizing my passion or my potential; I knew that.

I felt stuck. There was a yearning inside to break free. I didn't want to be the coffee girl forever.

On my lunch breaks, I bolted out of the office like a dog off-leash. The men in suits scurried away to their meetings as I cracked open my *Yoga Sutras* book and faded into my own little world.

11.36 Satya: For one established in truth, the result fits the action.

11.37 All the jewels appear for one who is firmly set in honesty.

Shit.

I shrank inside at the thought of telling my boss why I was leaving. *What if she thinks I abandoned her?* The day came when I found the courage to speak my authentic truth. To my surprise, she was supportive.

"Go live your dreams. Better things await you," she declared. My whole body settled into my chair. I sensed the mix of sadness and delight in her eyes, the way she was living vicariously through me.

I awoke each morning in the rainforest at 5:00 a.m. to the screeching sound of howler monkeys. In the afternoons, we gathered around the pool. My group was assigned to present Satya. *I can't believe it—divine alignment.*

I guided everyone to close down their eyes and feel the soles of their feet connected to the sun-warmed bricks. I invited them to come into their senses and settle deeper into their bodies:

"What does your inner truth feel like?"

I felt the movement of energy touching the hearts of our circle.

This is what I've come to this earth to share, guiding people to tap into

This body.

This breath.

Here, now.

The truth of this moment.

Inside of you.

My embodiment practices over the years have guided me into deep inner healing and authentic self-expression by allowing the full spectrum of me to feel seen, heard, and loved. The poems below are dedicated to acknowledging that desire and expressing the intention for how I hold sacred space for myself and others.

The Poems

Will You Love My Messy

Will you love my messy
Acknowledge my broken
See my wild, unbridled spirit
Dance with me barefoot under the moonlight
Will you show me your shame
Your insecurities, with the tears running down your face
in all the ways you have held yourself back from that which you truly desire
Will you tell me the stories of your scars
sitting around the crackling campfire
Let us take sledgehammers to the walls we've built up
See the playful child inside ourselves
Stare deep into one another's eyes
until we see nothing more than our own fragile humanity
Will you hear the parts of me that never felt safe to have a voice
Listen to her patiently and tenderly
Will you kiss me in all the right places
All the parts of me that didn't feel the love they so longed for
Can we celebrate in the beauty and vulnerabilities that makes us human
I do not want to live in a box
Painted pretty and admired by those who take the well-traveled path
Will you be the wind in my sails
So we may travel together to far and exotic places
To break free of all that we know
Shatter our world views and see everything through the eyes of a child
An insatiable curiosity that paints color across a grey sky
Looking within ourselves
and exploring the infinite possibilities of this existence
Show me your messy
The parts of yourself that are hidden away

that don't feel worthy of love
Let us fill those places together with laughter and compassion
Will you let me crack you open
and discover all the complexities that exist within you
The vulnerabilities, the heartache, the desires, the experiences
The unique emotional blueprint that is you
Will you let me shower you with love
Can we ride the waves of thinking we know ourselves
and savoring the mystery of knowing we are so much more
Can we dive deep inside ourselves
discovering the impressions from our past
Can you sit with me through the discomfort of the unknown
patiently, attentively to what is forming inside me
that which hasn't quite been put into words
Can you show me your weird
and I'll show you mine
so that we might remember what it is to play and create like children
That we might shed all the conditioning
naked and unafraid
and rediscover our true essence once again

I See You

I welcome you home
To your body, To your breath
To the rhythm of your unique heartbeat

Feel the pulse inside you
The aliveness
Here, Now

The sweet nectar of your own essence
The bare skin of your truth
The calling of your soul
Revealed
Moment by moment

Come home
You are held
All of you is welcome
Here
The sweet, soft sanctuary
Inside of you

I see You
All of you

Listen now
For the whispers
of who you are
Becoming

Dear Reader, now it's your turn to write. Use the space below. Don't censor yourself.

Bring your hand to your heart and connect with the rhythm of your breath. Ask yourself, "What does your inner truth feel like inside of you?"

Ashley Hall, RYT-500, is an expert yoga teacher and embodiment guide for transformative healing and self-discovery. Her gentle, explorative approach helps you compassionately unravel limiting patterns, realigned with your deepest truths, and move forward in flow. If you long to feel more heard and understood, Ashley's nurturing presence provides a space to listen deeply and access your inner knowing. By building body awareness, you can experience relief from tension and find alignment within yourself. Ashley's grounded guidance empowers you to tune into your body's profound wisdom to gain clarity, trust your intuition, and unlock your inner power. Begin your journey inward by downloading her free guide, Ignite Your Intuition https://www.inneralchemy.design/100poems

Chapter 20

A Healing Journey Through Community

Richard Bredeson

My Story

First assignment: turn seashells into beads, by hand, as personal offerings to the Holy! Crraackkk! My hand-held hammerstone, chosen for hardness and weight, comes down on the oyster shell, smashing it into shards of dull and shiny bits, some so small to be mere dust, others as large as a half-dollar. Yet among these bits and pieces of frozen ocean, I find a few about finger-nail size: perfect to shape into beads! Choosing one, I scrape the shard on my flat sandstone chosen for grinding to begin shaping it into a disk. I then use my hammerstone to knap a flake from a core of flint to create a sharp point (my hand tool) to drill the hole in the bead. The drilling is tough on fingers. I smell the salty ocean in the fine dust and sweat from the turning. Twisting and pressing with just the right touch, the hole appears—so satisfying. Smoothing all to finish, I have my first offering.

We sit together in a circle, pounding, grinding, shaping, and drilling shells into beads. This is Bolad's Kitchen, a virtual construction of an indigenous community created by Martín Prechtel, healer, shaman, story-holder, author, and most esteemed teacher who incites us to remember: "Remember the Holy who remember us remembering them!" I am looking for my indigenous soul, my journey of this lifetime.

How did I get here? Robert Bly, for me, the Master of the Mytho-Poetic Men's Movement, called me to the conference he held in northern Minnesota, a gathering of about a hundred men coming together to heal, sing, dance, read, and write poetry for each other. I had first met Robert at an earlier conference, A Day for Men, held in Washington, DC. Martín was to speak at The Minnesota Men's Conference.

I was flying to Minneapolis from Colorado on September 11, 2001; at the Colorado Springs airport, a crowd milled about in the lobby; planes had taken down the Twin Towers and took down my travel plans.

I did attend the 2002 Men's Conference and did meet Martín. It wasn't until 2008 that I found myself in Bolad's Kitchen shaping shells into beads to "feed the Holy" with our gifts of handwork, sweat, blistered fingers, and even a little blood: our puny sacrifices for the hope to reach for wholeness within the family of our fellow travelers.

We were a scraggly bunch from all over the world. But we were all here to learn and share, to listen to stories and solve riddles, to identify native music and make our own music, create our own stories and hold each other in a healing space of natural activities: constant bead-making, making shoes that gave humans the ability to walk long distances, shaping micaceous clay pots from native New Mexico quarries using Apache technology passed through generations, and above all, creating that space within the community and within ourselves to heal our wounded hearts.

We are all wounded; we are all healers. We all need community to nurture us on our journeys. I've been fortunate to have the incredible and indelible support of community throughout my entire life as I continue to seek, and often find, that indigenous healer-soul within. One of my many tools for healing is poetry: reading, writing, listening, speaking, creating the rhythms, and appreciating the sensual elements of the words. I learned the power of language at the feet of Robert Bly and in the Kitchen of Martín Prechtel; read aloud a Bly poem; pick up any of Martín's books; you'll hear exactly what I mean.

The Poems

I offer these poems created through my healing journey as a testament to the power of community to pull us, humanity, forward. Some are old; the first, "Honor Your Grandfather," was written in honor of Robert Bly and the first time I met him. The others are from other communities, both past and present. The last, "Human Virtues," is from a book on "Circular Leadership," the governing model for "A Community of Transformation," of which I am currently a member.

Honor Your Grandfather

The clear day was filled
With heightened expectations—
"A Day for Men."

At the entrance we were guided
Through a side door leading to steps
Descending into the womb of the theater.

As we wound through narrow passages
Voices whispered: "Remember your Grandfather,"
"Remember the Ancestors," "Honor your Father."

A faint rumble echoed
At the edge of perception—it began
To resolve into rhythm.

Dark warmth held us, then
Suddenly we were birthed
Onto a stage amidst fifty men.

Drumming! Dancing! We were urged on--
Asked to dance across the stage,
To perform for the sea of faces witnessing.

The short trip was filled
With tension—light, sound, motion
Blending in splendid cacophony.

Off stage, at our seats, we stood
Dancing in place, pounding rhythm
Of drums, hands, feet driving.

"Remember your Grandfather" echoed
On the rhythm. He appeared on stage
Larger than he had ever been in life.

Tears flowed—"He would have loved this!"
Primeval sensation drove his body
And mine as we entrained with the drum.

Remembered days with him—the
Dark Tavern—blue smoke hanging
Sullenly in the sodden air.

The bar supporting elbows
Of overcalled farmers—fresh manure still
Clinging to rubbered boots.

The sweet/sour whiskey and beer breaths
Mingled with aimless talk
Of weather, crops and cows.

They laughed and cried, shared lies
That covered their fears and
Broken dreams—we laughed, cried.

The almost painful rhythm
Brought back the now—then stopped!
We had arrived.

A Speculation on Perfection

Someone once asked me:
"What if the world is perfect
Just the way it is?"
Pause, breathe, what if!

Cosmologists say we are in a perfect
State of balance for consciousness
To rise and recognize Self, Light.
Pause, breathe, what if!

A trillion neutrinos hit every second,
A trillion stars pulse in Andromeda,
Three trillion trees support the Earth.
Pause, breathe, what if!

One hundred trillion synapses
In the human brain awaken connections
Across the Universe, flash to awareness.
Pause, breathe, what if!

Light and dark in balance, perfection.
Love and consciousness awake and aware.
One hundred billion humans passing this way.
Pause, breathe, what if!

Imagine perfection; I know you can.
This is our Universe filled with Light and Love.
We made this through our connections.
Pause, breathe, what if!

My Life as a Poem

Waking to my day, a new page,
The threads of a dream drift away
On the winds of another life,
A poem gone now, glimpsed, forgotten.

Today a new dream begins, a new
Story of my own creating,
Speaking to the future, trusting in
The worthiness of these words.

Practice, it all begins and ends there.
Story is practice, a moving toward
Perfection, evolving with a rhythm;
Sometimes involving a rhyme.

With repetition the story resolves
Into a poem: my life as a poem.
For slips and slights I practice
Forgiveness – changing my perception.

Sometimes the words don't come,
Resisting the page refusing to flow.
For the hesitance, the lurches I practice
Patience – waiting on the muse.

Regretting all that I have lost, resenting
What has been taken or misplaced;
For the destruction and death I practice
Praise – remembering life is ecstatic!

The suffering millions weigh heavily on my heart;
Stafford got it right when he said:
"The darkness around us is deep." I practice
Compassion – wanting to save with my words.

These words may not be worthy as those of
The Bard of Stratford-upon-Avon. Yet, I read
And weep and rejoice and sing. And I practice
Wisdom – moving toward the light.

For all the grace, the wisdom, the compassion
I reach for words to reflect the deep.
I look up at the moon and practice
Gratitude – knowing they'll appear complete.

At the end of the day, practice done
I realize I have one more line to
Write, one from my heart; and I practice
Love – the Love Poem of My Life.

Human Virtues

Love:
It all begins with love,
The creating force alive
Through the whole world
From deepest deep to highest above.

Honor:
A state of being derived from love,
Self-love, the source of all;
A principle that upholds, ennobles,
Creating the foundation for Human.

Integrity:
Springing from honor, Human
Knows place in the world; holds
Space firmly on that foundation;
Rises to each occasion to bless.

Community:
Integral Human reaches outward
To serve humanity in blessed community.
Community blesses Human in sacred symmetry
Echoing voices of goddesses and gods.

High Purpose:
The highest purpose is to love,
Honor, grow in integrity, serve
Community in a spiral blessing rising
Through the evolution of Humanity.

Dear reader, now it's your turn to write! Use the space below. Don't censor yourself.

Where have you found your healing community?

Richard Bredeson is a healer and technology expert. Retired from a 40-year career in the aerospace and communications industry, he is now self-employed with his wife, Rosemary Robertson Bredeson, The Scientific Mystic, in businesses to bring their healing talents to the world. He develops and maintains websites for their businesses and other organizations. Richard is ordained as an Interfaith Minister by *The School of Sacred Ministries, Doylestown,* PA. He and Rosemary provide "spiritual services" through their *Church of A New Alliance,* Inc., a non-profit organization. Richard researches, practices, and teaches Qigong, an ancient Chinese approach to health, happiness, and longevity. He is a member and webmaster for A Community of Transformation. He published chapters in two best-selling books: *Circular Leadership: Together We Rise* and *The Ultimate Guide to Self-Healing, Volume 2.* Richard sporadically publishes thoughts and poems on his blog, https://menandthegoddess.com/

Find his community at: https://ChurchofANewAlliance.org

Chapter 21

Letting Love Lead – Living a Life of Freedom, Love, and Joy

Yantra-ji, Therapist, Artist, Author, Spiritual Teacher

As I sit here now
I ponder what changes us
Only Love does that

My Story

I never thought I'd be a widow at the age of twenty-one with a child, living back at the home I needed to get away from, in order to find space for myself to live, love, and breathe.

We were so different, Mum and I. She was too big, bright, loud, needy, weepy, angry, and emotional after the divorce from Dad, and at times suffocating me with her love. I was small, shy, quiet, self-contained, and unemotional, although fearful and very private. A clashing of two worlds, a mother needing love and a daughter trying to get away from it.

Sitting on the opposite side of the room to Mum, I was doing some written exercises, based on the Biblical principles of forgiveness, seventy times for seven days (Matthew 18:21-22 KJV). Line after line, day after day, I wrote it out:

I forgive my mum—no I don't.

I forgive my mum—I can't.

I'd pause and look up: *Is she looking at me? No.*

I'd keep writing:

I forgive my mum—I want to.

I forgive my mum—okay.

Until:

I forgive my mum—yes.

At the time, Mum never knew what I was doing, but in living at home, grieving with my one-year-old after the death of her dad, something needed to heal, and I was willing. Forgiveness transformed the pain, hurt, and hate of my early life into love.

Years later, this love enabled me to be there for Mum through my divorce, which resulted in her losing her home, supporting her through her dementia journey and the death of my teenage son. During that time Mum had a fall and was in rehab; we were visiting her.

"Where's Cohen?" she asked innocently. I looked wide-eyed in shock, from Mum to my hubby and daughter and back to Mum again.

"Mum," I said, with tears in my eyes, my voice quavering, and my body starting to shake, "Coey died. You came with us to his funeral." It was heartbreaking telling her like it was the first time—the shock, pain, and tears all over again. I take a deep breath now as I write this, and my heart is clenching like it did then. Love is what enables us to do the hard things.

After the death of my son, I used writing for healing, to get up and out of me what was occurring, words that needed to be said and later shared. Over the years, these words have become a lifeline of simple honesty for myself and others as they strip away the unessential.

There's a simplicity to the truth revealed in poetry. There's a way we can experience, feel, and hear the naked truth expressed. It allows what might be difficult to write or express to become simple, stripped down, and pared back to the essential. Poetry removes the non-essential, allowing me to share about death and loss and life and love.

Poetry leaves space
For the finding of oneself
In between the words

Anyone can pause for a moment and become still and silent; we don't need to be an author or poet to write or create. Poetry is a kind of undoing. It's all God's grace doing this undoing, and we heal in this embrace. It's the simplicity of the heart, the silence of the space between life and mind and heart and God that allows the words to flow—here is where we let love lead.

The Poems

My Mum - Yes That Too Is Love

She birthed me, held me, fed me—yes that is love—the bond of a mother and baby

She disciplined me, protected me, controlled me—yes that too is love—showing me which boundaries are mine and which are not

She cared for me, helped me, guided me—yes that is love—through actions

She feared me, envied me, resented me—yes that too was love—showing her about herself through me, what was hers and what was not

She let me go my own way—yes that is love—allowing space for our relationship to grow

She wanted me, needed me, suffocated me—yes that too was love—teaching that love breathes

She held my hands as I birthed my own baby—yes that is love—one mother guiding another

She was fierce and protective of her pride—yes that too was love—as she learnt what hurt her own heart

She heard me, listened to me, let me in—yes that is love—trusting, deepening, allowing

She needed attention, craved it, wanted it—yes that too was love—teaching her she was already enough

She cuddled and snuggled and read to and cared for all of my children—yes that is love—being open and available to give and receive

She was open and closed, opening and closing—yes that too was love—as we learnt the value of trusting the truth together

She laughed and joked and was the life of the party—yes that is love—sharing her joy

She needed reassurance, reminding, re-telling—yes that too was love—being revealed through patience

She cried with me as we said goodbye to my son—yes that is love—through sharing heartbreak and pain

She forgot and remembered and forgot and remembered—yes that too is love—through understanding, gentle reminders and to laugh at it all

She needed me, this time our roles were reversed—yes that is love—allowing me to be surrendered to her, to love, to who she is

She felt confronted, afraid and alone—yes that too is love—as she allowed herself to be held, soothed, comforted

She trusted me—yes that is love—one heart opening to another

She allowed me to meet her fully, loving her just as she was—yes that is love—innocent, fresh and free

She took her last breath with her favorite granddaughter holding her hand and all of us in her room—yes that too is love—the willingness to let go in total surrender

She flashes in my memory, as I get ready to sleep—yes that is love—as my tears drop upon the pillow

She is the preciousness still sweet in my heart, now many years ago today—yes that too is love—as I surrender and allow it all

My mum—yes all is this endless love

These words written after Mum's passing in 2016 are both a snippet and a lifetime of love.

She

A poem written for International Women's Day.

She started off perfect, whole, genderless
Then the form folded, molded and became she
Floating in her perfect world
in the womb of woman
surrounded by the warmth
the embrace and love of 'She'

Birthed into the world, she was seen
acknowledged, recognized
Gender was seen, named, in the world around
No longer was she seen as just herself
Yet She was still perfect, whole, genderless

There was no sense of identity
No sense of conformity
just flesh and blood, bone and love
Yes love, for that is who she is and was

Yet the world continued to pour into her
The ideas of self, the ideas of she
the ideas of her
the ideas of woman
Struggling to be, these ideas took hold

Even though, She was still perfect, whole, genderless
She believed the lie
that she was form
that she was identity
that she was now this 'She'

A life was grown, built, demolished
and grown and built again
Time and time again she found herself
constructing her life, her roles
believing herself to be this idea
this one, this she, this her, this woman

Crashing again and again against the tide
of what she knew herself to be
always perfect, whole, genderless
the truth was never lost
just pushed into the background

Her heart whispered – hear me, know me, love me
hear yourself, know yourself, love yourself
Her life kept reflecting
love and pain, joy and hate, war and peace
What could she trust in the outward expression
of 'She'?

At first she wanted to kick and scream, to rebel
She wanted to be this idea, this her
this she, this woman
Slowly she listened to her heart
to this love that was swooning within her

The ruthless voice of truth arose within
It showed her everything she was not
everything that was not her
everything that was not woman
She was still perfect, whole, genderless

She listened, she softened, she surrendered
and here she found herself
Here all along
Even though the wild ride of her life
pointed to her as someone, she saw the truth
That her, she, woman, was just an idea

She was still perfect, whole, genderless
Instead of an idea
She discovered that the whole of the universe
was contained within her
created and birthed through her
Lived here and now, as her

She let the sacredness of life, live her
Be her, fill her, become her
Then her life became an offering of love
A dance of love, a tune of love
Her body became a temple of love

Every fold, molded and curved
became the truth of her
Form or formless no longer defined her
This that she is, here and now
always had been
and always will be

Even after the last breath
breathed in and breathed out
This one – that was seen, known
and lived as 'She'
always perfect, whole, genderless

In deepest gratitude for the blessing of this life in form.

Loves Hand

Often, we imagine that love is a feeling, that love is nice, that love will let us off the hook, that to be free, we won't have to feel. Love's hand will lead us, love has its own ideas, if we will but trust and follow love's lead—are you willing?

Stop she says - No I'm busy
Stop she says - No I can't
Stop she says - No I don't want to
Yes she says, I know
but for the truth, you are willing
So, yes I stop.

With stopping
comes the unbearable
the pain, heartbreak
comes like an unexpected
unwelcome visitor
One who is uninvited
Demanding to stay
Demanding attention
Demanding notice.

Who wants to go there?
Down into the pit
When it doesn't feel like love
doesn't feel real,
doesn't feel like this
bleakness will end.

Even when you're spent
When there is nothing more
to give, nothing left
Still demanding more
As the chest heaves
and aches.

The fingers
of unbearable hurt
Pain, despair
Agony
Clawing at the chest
Clawing at the breath
Clawing at your very life
Wanting still more.

Like a wild animal
that won't be subdued
won't be silenced
Until you give

every last drop of
your blood, your breath
your life.

And then –
in that instant
there is light
Weightless
the heart beats
the lungs breathe
The life that is here
filled with the glowing
pulse of freedom.

Untainted
Slowly unfurling
glowing
A smile comes.

How could anything
have seemed so bleak
when it was love's hand
all along
Clawing you back
into herself
so she can claim you
fully
finally.

Yes – I surrender
I am hers
And she is mine
As we have been
All along.

The Truth of Love

This is a poem I wrote a few years ago titled 'The Truth of Love' - Whatever your word for love—Love is All.

Whatever your word for love – love fully
fall at the feet of love
drown in love
love is the One beloved

If God is your word for love – love fully
Love with all of your heart
Pray in love, meditate on love, open to all as love

Whatever your word for love – love fully
love endlessly
love with devotion

If consciousness is your word for love – love fully
Love with awareness
Be the flame, the light of love

Whatever your word for love – love fully
fall at the feet of love
drown in love
love is the beloved

If Grace is your word for love – love fully
Love softly, sweetly, openly
Trust this that is love

Whatever your word for love – love fully
love endlessly
love with devotion

If Jesus is your word for love – love fully
Be led by the hand of love
Let love be alive in your heart

Whatever your word for love – love fully
fall at the feet of love
drown in love
love is the beloved

If Presence is your word for love – love fully
Love with your full attention
Let love permeate all

Whatever your word for love – love fully
love endlessly
love with devotion

If the Divine is your word for love – love fully
Swim in love
Dance in the ecstasy of love

Whatever your word for love – love fully
fall at the feet of love
drown in love
love is the beloved

If Mother, Father, Lover, Other, is your word for love – love fully
Love fiercely, love freely, love passionately
Cherish love in form

Whatever your word for love – love fully
love endlessly
love with devotion

If Forgiveness is your word for love – love fully
Stay open in love
Surrendered in love

Whatever your word for love – love fully
fall at the feet of love
drown in love
love is the beloved

If All, Self, Freedom, Silence, This, is your word for love – love fully
Be the totality of love
Love the totality of all

Whatever your word for love – love fully
love endlessly
love with devotion

If Life is your word for love – love fully
Live fully in love, laugh in love, cry in love
Share in love, receive in love
Live the truth of love

Whatever your word for love – love fully
fall at the feet of love
drown in love
love is the One beloved

Whatever your word for love - Love is All

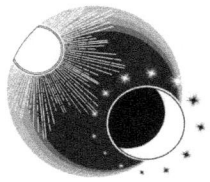

Dear Reader, now it's your time to write! Use the blank space. Don't censor yourself.

Pause for a moment, take a breath and let yourself become still and silent, as you hold the pen in your hand, allow your heart to open and the words to flow – here, is where you let love lead...

Yantra-ji is a facilitator of True Self-Inquiry, a senior practitioner of The Journey Method, teacher of The Enneagram, and creator of The Myth of Fixation Discovering True Freedom Enneagram retreat, Spiritual Teacher, Therapist, Speaker, Artist, Illustrator and Author of 10 published books.

My commitment is to support you in the realization of the truth of who you are – regardless of gender, form, identity, life, or circumstances – this that you are is always here, fresh, present, and free in every moment. In meeting together, there is the opportunity to ask deeper questions; through stillness and inquiry, we come to know the truth—that we are totally free in this very moment now.

If we haven't yet met together in-person or online, I encourage you to book a free call with me. In our meeting together, we will discover how I may be of true support to you.

Living Alignment Website
https://www.LivingAlignment.com

Chapter 22

5 Ways to be Unstoppable After Divorce

Miko Reed

My Story

As we were waiting for our next assignments, I glanced around the small auditorium. I noticed a group of soldiers to the left of me, eyes dancing at my smile. I knew I had their attention. Some of us soldiers were sent to other units at Walter Reed, while others, like myself, were sent to the Naval Base in Virginia Beach for EMT training. Little did I know I'd end up marrying and having two beautiful children with one of them.

What started off as flirty fun and excitement ended up being a lifelong waltz of push and pull and complete compromise on my end. I gave up all of my friends and assimilated with his circle. I gave up my dreams of writing and became a full-time mom, wife, and soldier. And before I knew it, 16 years passed. I had a big house in the suburbs, traveled out of the country once or twice a year, had a nice car, adorable kids (a girl and a boy), and seemingly a doting husband. So, according to social media standards, I'd made it.

While I was completely financially provided for and a huge participant in the financial aspects of the household, so many intangibles were missing. This is something we knew around year 13, yet we stayed, possibly out of convenience, possibly out of fear of the unknown. We were barely talking, and it seemed as if the entire house was on eggshells. What looked vibrant and aesthetically pleasing on social media was indeed the opposite in real life. We were caretakers and museum workers, meaning we took care of the kids and ensured our home was impeccable, but our souls suffered immensely. We were rote.

As 2019 rolled around, my medical issues forced me into an early retirement from the Army. I was also nearing the end of my Graduate program at Georgetown University. There was excitement in the air for us both—a fresh start, new beginnings? I was slated to begin a new civilian job, and we agreed to start therapy. Then, enter March 2020.

As the Pandemic set in, my marriage was met with many challenges we were unable to withstand. Marriage is hard; divorce is hard, and that sentence can end with a definite period. While I was heartbroken, I will say that everyone deserves to be happy.

Now, what are five ways you can become unstoppable after a divorce? For starters:

1. Forgive yourself and forgive your mate.
2. Figure it out and have faith that your life after divorce will work out. Allow yourself time to process.
3. Focus. Write it out. Go to therapy. Meditate. Revisit old passions and hobbies. Spend time with your kids
4. Fortify yourself while you grieve. After sharing your life with someone, it's important that you recognize that grieving is

normal. Give yourself grace and allow yourself time to cry and be angry, to feel defeated and ruminate.

5. Fearless, fabulous, and free: Get up and *start moving!* Meet new people. Connect with friends. Love yourself again. Picture the future and shape your life.

The Poems

When I started writing about the breakdown of my marriage, I felt broken and defeated. I realized that in order to move forward, I had to let my vulnerability take the lead. When I did that, I was able to address my fears.

I'm Scared of Dying

I'm scared of dying
Not in the way that you may think
Not in the car accident or plane crashing way
Let me be frank.
Like scared of dying while alive
Alive and still dead
Still.
Like crocodiles hovering under shallow waters at the cusp of dawn
Imminent death
Alive
Like volcanos on the edge of eruption
Fire brewing inside
Dead
Like I'm a walking talking shell of myself
Of what I'm capable of
Of my joys
Of my dreams
Alive.
I'm scared of being too scared to be free
That I'm going to be drowned by my inner history
You know, the one that shaped me
The one that I tried to keep a mystery
Too scared to recreate me
I'm scared of dying y'all

Of being alive and not being able to see
But seeing the old me
Watch the new me
Easy like the breeze
Easy like a cover girl
Carefree
Like a cloud, far-away in the sky
Untouchable
I'm scared of dying
While alive

This was my first time saying "out loud" that I was scared of dying. I felt heard. I understood my plight more. I truly believe that in order to start the healing process you have to be honest with yourself and address your fears head on. Then I reflected on what was. I vented and unpacked my feelings of what it felt like now that my marriage was ending, through my words.

What Happens When A Marriage Is Ending (Part 1)

When a marriage is ending you feel catatonic
Often compared to death or the grief of a death, or a dazed haze
But a death nonetheless
A stupor
A coma
You feel as if your head is spinning while you talk to the kids and try to explain shit you don't even understand yourself
Brain dead

You speculate over the one- hundred "what ifs"
Days and nights run together
Gotta smile while you face it all
Your group chat is nervous
They feel the pain
Effortless
Of your fall
Cumbersome
Your circle becomes smaller, because lines are drawn
And one day, while you're sipping mimosas and cleaning out the closets, you gasp
(By the way you're always gasping when a marriage is ending)
This time you buckle at your knees and think, ahhh yes, this is the time for dramatics
You chuckle at your sick wit in the midst of this cyclone
Your wedding album falls out and baby's first birthday album comes tumbling down right behind it
Yep, Mercury is in retrograde
A picture with a happy quatro follows
You gasp
And while you pour yourself more champagne you open the Burn Book, now aptly titled, and wonder where the years have went
You hold back tears
(By the way you're always holding back tears when a marriage is ending)
You pick up your phone and respond to the demands of your group chat with an unnecessary sharpness
They gasp
"It's been 6 months," they say
I look at the calendar, fucking no way
They're right
The expectation that I should be over this marriage ending lingers in the air
As if 17 years
Nothing
As if I don't deserve grace
Nevermind
They don't get it
The closet, back to the burn book in the closet

My belief is this: take whatever time you feel is needed to process, grieve, live alone and start to learn yourself; then get to healing and living your life, in all of its glorious abundance. You have to find someone that accepts you, as you begin to accept yourself, in all states, broken, happy, funny, depleted, and whole…let that be the goal.

This Love

The one that catches me will know that I want to be caught
He will travel to the highest elevation of the stratosphere
And marvel at the copious constellations
He will name the most beautiful one Oshun and place it on the axis
of my heart
The one that catches me will massage my soul- and mix it with his
ambiance
Until we blend
Like an Italian love dish- but black
We be tiramisu and sweet potato pie
He will love me with every inch of my broken
And together- together we will pour our dreams out over poetry
And gently slather them across the Southern borders of Nigeria
Fuse them in tandem during tantric breathing
Our dreams
Cultivate them through meditation, reiki healings and therapy
This love will stick to our souls like the good old days
To our bones like a fresh down goose on winter mornings.
This love
Like mamas slow cooked brisket on Easter Sunday
This love will drizzle down on spectators like Vibranium
Necessary absorption
Like the soft feel of morning dew on famished soil
We will stretch our arms across the Mozambique Greenlands and dip

our fingertips into the South African Coastline-summoning the spirits
of our ancestors-with this love
We will scribe sonnets for each other and tuck them in the crevices of
earth's equator-so we may find them in our dreams at night.
The one that catches me will speak eternity on the tip of his tongue
He will breathe me in and
hold my mortality in his esophagus
He will tell me that he's consuming it whole to rebirth a new story for
us
Untarnished
Bold
Where we love each other carefully
Intentionally
And we will intoxicate each other with the purest form of agape
He will place my face in his hands and kiss the four quadrants and
whisper "baby-fuck those other people-it's just us."
And imma believe it this time.
The one that catches me will hold me in his embrace-while I read
sonnets- inside the crevices of earth's equator-while we sleep
Ase'

Now, this was done over a two year span, hence the phrase, give yourself
grace. I also read other artists' work and took advice when I saw that it
offered a benefit. I hope you will be able to connect to some of these pieces
and know that your worth is not attached to the end of a marriage, as this
is merely a chapter in the story of your beautiful life.

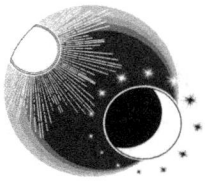

Dear reader, now it's your turn to write. Use the space below. Don't censor yourself.

If your spouse lost their memory, what's the first thing you would tell them about your relationship and about the love you share? What's the second?

Miko Reed is a native Washingtonian, retired Army Master Sergeant, and has been writing poetry for over 20 years. She is an author, public speaker, curator and host. Miko completed her Executive Masters in Leadership from Georgetown University in 2019, started her company Have A Voice, LLC, in 2020, and became an Amazon bestselling author of *Eggshells In Soft Black Hands* in August 2021.

Miko has also been published in various publications, including Bourgeon magazine 2023, an international anthology, *Now that you are Gone From This World,* and The Journal of Expressive Writing, both in 2022. Her second book, a novelette of fiction, titled *Pandemic- Suburban Women,* was completed in the Fall of 2022. Miko is working on her 3rd book of poetry and prose titled *Pain & Prosecco,* slated for completion in November 2023. Miko is a mom of two beautiful kids. Connect with Miko Reed at: http://mikoreed.com

Chapter 23

From Unsure I'd Survive to Learning to Thrive

Michol Mae Tuttle, MSc

My Story

I'm Michol Mae, and if I had a dollar for every time someone called me "over-sensitive" I'd be rich. My sensitivity, compassion, and empathy became my superpower when I finally learned how to harness them. My experiences shifted from something to overcome to an opportunity to help someone.

I have experienced tremendous loss, abuse, and life-changing moves. These events challenged me to research the tools I could use and share with others who might need them. I embarked on an apprenticeship for shamanism and currently continuously obtain certifications for sound healing and guiding meditations. I found Martial Arts, Journeying, and Meditation among the most powerful tools for healing yourself and others.

My journey to heal and help others started when I was a very young child with a few types of childhood abuse. It continued with sexual assaults as a teenager and a few abusive relationships. I lost my mother at the age of fifteen. Both men she chose to be my father abandoned me at different times. This abandonment sometimes caused me to feel like an orphan.

I was frequently underestimated; those who don't come from much often are. When my mother sent me to live with my biological father, I lived with eight additional people in a three-bedroom apartment, sleeping on one of two couches. I was traumatized and sensitive; no one expected anything but failure.

Life with my father was a complete 180 from life with my mom, where she expected perfection in school, music, and every other area. Despite, or out of spite, perhaps a little of both, I continued to become the first person in my family to receive a Master's Degree. I did my best to help raise my siblings, later taking in two children from one of my siblings to keep the children from foster care.

Knowing what it was like to find out your dad was really your stepdad, and feeling the pain of being treated less than the other children, I decided to love them as if they were my own. I chased them around the house when they were cranky, yelling, "You just need more love," and hugged them when I caught them. Sadly, all the love I had wasn't enough for my boy; he chose to take his life the year before the pandemic. I lost everything. I wasn't sure I could survive. Initially, I survived for my girl. I knew she didn't deserve a living-dead parent. I learned I wasn't an artist, singer, or writer anymore. My entire identity became being their parent. I learned so much about grief, healing, and mindfulness to survive. Now, I've moved forward in my journey, intent to set up the best tool belt to thrive.

You believed the light
within extinguished but it's
an eternal flame.

The Poems

Curiously Common

It's a curious thing to know so many suffered as I did.
How could something so brutal become so common?

Molded and shaped to accept brutish behavior and make excuses,
I remember feeling I couldn't possibly recover from the abuses.

Childhood scars seemed to dictate my actions without my understanding,
Propelling me into more situations that would further scar me.

The alternative was to embrace it and become what they called me,
And embrace the abuse, their definition, and the depravity.

It is interesting looking back after trauma therapy has succeeded,
From a lens that isn't jaded or warped or misleading.

I deserved love, yes. But. I deserved to learn to love myself.
Yet, I struggled for most of my life figuring this out.

The risk of overcorrecting and becoming jaded was real,
I didn't want to be bitter and hateful; a balance would be ideal.

But my mistrust for the type of people that had taken so much,
Often led to me putting up walls and using them as a crutch.

It was easier for me to isolate myself than to put myself out there,
And risk being wrong and end up in another nightmare.

After a few failed attempts at finding healthy relationships,
I put everything on hold until I could heal more from this.

As I healed and learned more about loving myself authentically,
I started to set standards and learn healthy boundaries.

I learned it isn't selfish to put your needs over someone's wants,
And taking care of yourself starts with your own thoughts.

I slowly began to learn more about self-compassion,
And how to talk to myself with more affection.

The truth is if you wouldn't say the same things to someone you care for,
Then you don't deserve to have them said to you anymore.

Next, I leaned in on gratitude practices daily,
Finding three things to be grateful for should be easy.

I learned the subtle art of self-forgiveness,
No small feat for a devout perfectionist.

I learned I need people around me that want to grow,
Because I will never stop wanting to learn more.

There was a time I wasn't sure I could ever survive,
But now I know we all have it in us to rise.

So, I added another assignment of my own free will,
To find three things I loved about myself daily until,

Until I knew without a doubt I was worthy of my own protection,
And I was worthy of a love that offered meaningful connection.

I felt the peace within my soul scream out wanting more,
Finally, I knew the life I dreamed of was, in fact, possible.

I didn't want a fairytale, I didn't have unrealistic expectations,
I wanted a deeper level of love with emotional intelligence.

Even with this knowledge, I was still secure and safe in my solitude,
Now I know it's more important to give the love you crave back to you.

Overcoming Abuse

They taught me by the tender age of six,
That a girl or woman's ultimate value is sex,
Then again, when I was entering my teens at thirteen,
I learned what it was like to freeze under a man of eighteen.

He had a good time; I'm sure he assumed I did too,
But my mind had floated off while my body resumed,
I went home to shower when all was said and done
Took a razor and cut my face, my mind still stunned.

It seemed like the earlier abuse marked me for more,
Like a beacon, I didn't know I had, calling to its source,
As if somehow they knew I was a damaged easy mark
Because again at seventeen things got infinitely more hard.

I made excuses through all the years about these men,
But a forty-year-old has no business with teenaged children
Abuse wasn't designated to men significantly older in age
The verbal, physical, or sexual abuse was present, regardless of who I'd date.

They say if you are the common denominator it's probably you,
So I tried my best to do more healing, to stop future abuse,
And I learned a little more about what not to accept each time,
Still, I found myself having to heal more wounds after each guy.

I was a strong and independent woman, so I shouldn't fall prey to abuse,
So everyone seemed to think, along with it won't happen to you,
Obviously, no one would have chosen someone abusive if they knew,
But our brains are wired chemically to ignore red flags when it's new.

The reality is an abuser rarely shows their true colors in the beginning,
Sometimes the abuse isn't even the result of a bad person scheming,
Sometimes it's incompatibility that isn't realized until you're too far in
As you both try to be perfect for each other, wanting the relationship to win.

Overtime the fights begin, accompanied by an erosion of self,
Happening so slowly you remain unaware of the dangers, or need for help
Like the frog in the pot of water, you can't feel the temperature rise,
Everyone outside can see you cooking, but you think everything is fine.

Perhaps, toxicity comes from trying to force an incompatible match,
And we need not label the person, toxic, abusive, terrible, or bad.
While acknowledging they are bad or toxic for us pursuing the life we deserve,
And moving forward taking with us everything we have learned.

But, how do we turn off the beacon that was activated when we were young?
How do we tell our brain not to ignore the red flags as we move on?
By unlearning a lot of detrimental subconscious lessons that were taught
Inflicted by other broken persons damaging us with little to no thought.

The journey will be individual to each person who chooses the path,
And healing can be difficult but it's something we deserve to have,
We won't be robbed of a life of happiness because of others evil deeds,
We will rise from the ashes of our trauma and become all we are meant to be.

Learning Grief

Society can be cruel to the grieving heart,
They say to get over it before the healing can start,
And so many people busy their grief away,
I was one of them until the most tragic of days.

My grief journey started when I was eleven years old,
It probably started before then, but that's how memory goes,
My dear Nana and Papa fell ill around the same time,
Although we did everything we could we couldn't stop the tide

I was a bit too young to understand the emotions that I felt,
And again I seemed to struggle with grief when my dad left,
But society doesn't give us time and space to breathe,
And it doesn't consider all the different types of grief.

So I just buried the feelings deep down inside,
And when, at thirteen, my mom sent me away I cried
Later when the anger surfaced I didn't think it was grief,
Because handling grief wasn't something anyone taught me.

At fifteen when she died of the plague we call cancer,
the swirl of emotions was destined to lead me to disaster.
Still, I had no real valuable grief education to lean upon
So I floundered about trying everything and anything to move on.

When my grandmother died her words echoed through my mind,
Think positive and positive things will happen, I felt purpose stir inside,
I coped with her death by starting my very own experiment,
I would honor her by testing the words that became my inheritance.

It seemed to me every couple of years yet another person died,
And I continued to busy away my grief convinced I was fine.
One day we lost my precious cousin, a teen, to suicide,
I found even more things to busy away the time.

The grief still found its way in and I found the four agreements,
A book that seemed to save me from my state of bereavement.
I embarked on another phase of my journey, shifting my mind
I leaned more heavily into healing as I busied away more time.

I thought I was a pro, there was no loss that would make me backslide
Until the most tragic of days, I lost my own teen to suicide.
Despite all my research and healing nothing had prepared this time,
I felt like the darkness would consume me forever, I'd forever lost my light.

I didn't just lose my child that day, I lost so much more
This grief was heavier and deeper than anything I'd experienced before
I sold my home because I couldn't go back to the place he died,
I lost my sense of security, I lost my own internal flame inside.

Out of my greatest darkness, grief, and despair came a deeper understanding,
With intentional choice and hard work healing, I felt my knowledge expanding,
Suddenly, I realized I never really learned how to process my grief fully
I learned it came in waves, and society would be my greatest bully.

Everyone will experience their grief journey uniquely and at their own pace.
A safe person is someone who will be there holding a safe space.
When the grief bursts hit it's okay to sit with it or lean into the waves,
They won't last forever, but I do remember them lasting for days.

I hate the saying, "It gets easier with time." it seems like a lie,
You get stronger as you add more tools to your tool belt you can apply,
When you think your flame is gone, just feed it the healing spark to ignite,
And that internal flame we all have, is eternal, it will always be inside.

Transformed

I thought I couldn't survive this…
How could I? It's too horrendous.
The loss of a child, seeing him lifeless
There is no possible way I can survive this.

All the light I was made up of had gone dark
My flame, my inner light, extinguished, gone
I'll never smile or laugh, or feel joy again
How could I ever feel any of that after losing him?

Someone told me, a few months after,
Happiness is a choice, Your happiness matters,
But I didn't choose this, I rebelled against the thought
He chose this and the world as I know it is gone.

But I continued my path, trying to heal, for her,
She still needed a parent, more than ever, I was sure,
Healing was hard, and I was told more than once,
Life is for the living, and I deserved love.

Assigned a gratitude assignment I balked,
I found it hard to be grateful for anything at all.
I would have given him my last breath, after all.
I couldn't even be grateful for breathing, so I started small.

I was grateful for my girl, my pets, and my experience of being mindful,
I was grateful I still found the sun, the moon, and the stars tranquil,
Some days I was grateful a stranger smiled, or said something hopeful,
For my resilience, my healing, and my compassion, I was grateful.

I didn't think this assignment would do much for me at the time,
But I was dedicated to it, and perhaps the assigner was right.
I used to do this regularly, but it was harder to see the gratitude this time,
Still, the more I looked for things to be grateful for the more I could find.

Suddenly, it was there, that flicker of light inside.
I had to continue my healing, I had to give it a try,
Was it possible the flame inside hadn't truly died?
Was it possible, this was something I could survive?

By the third year, I could smile and even laugh once more,
It was clear I couldn't simply be who I was before,
And though I was still on a journey to find my new norm,
I had survived once again, I wasn't the same, I was transformed.

Dear reader, now it's your turn to write. Use the space below. Don't censor yourself.

Write about your rise! If you get stuck, try some writing about gratitude and self-love!

Michol Mae is the founder of Lady Mae Impressions and a talented artist, author, educator, poet, and musician. She weaves her wisdom, experiences, practice, and knowledge of meditation, shamanism, and sound and energy healing into her poetry, music, and novels as a way to combat abuse, trauma, and grief and help others feel less alone on their journey and normalize mental health. Michol loves all furry friends, and you'll find her cat, Mac Lir, on her social media. Connect with Michol on her website: https://www.ladymaeimpressions.com

Chapter 24

A Path Forward: Hatred's Antidote in Unity

Jacqueline Solimini, MPH

My Story

Growing up in a mid-sized city, I always believed hatred and prejudice were distant concepts that only existed in history books. That perception was shattered one fateful day when an incident occurred that changed my life forever.

It was a sunny afternoon, and the local green was bustling with activity. Children played with family and other kids nearby, couples reclined on blankets enjoying lunch, and people walking or jogging exchanged warm greetings. Amidst this serene weekend scene, a troubling incident unfolded. A group of individuals arrived and began hurling offensive slurs and hateful remarks at a family who had recently moved to the area. Their words were like venom, poisoning the air and creating an atmosphere of tension and fear.

Witnessing this blatant display of hatred was both shocking and heart-wrenching. As I looked around, I noticed a mix of reactions from the bystanders. Some seemed uncomfortable but chose to look away, while others wore expressions of disbelief. At that moment, I felt a surge of emotions: anger at the perpetrators, sadness for the targeted family, and a deep sense of disappointment in my community.

Throughout the world, hatred and prejudice between people and within communities, cultures, religions, and nations refuse to die. Hatred is a vicious cycle confirming how thinking and actions work in tandem to produce disharmony. Reflecting on the topic of hatred, I realized that combating hatred is not only about confronting the perpetrators; it is about fostering a culture of empathy, education, and understanding. All of us play a role, no matter how small the effort or futile the outcome may seem. Even in the face of darkness, a single candle of kindness and compassion can illuminate an inclusive and harmonious discourse and path in society.

We must not accept the errant premise that hatred is an unfortunate byproduct of societal groupings or a fait accompli where we simply throw up our hands in frustration and sadly lament that some people are just born this way, with no alternative for unity. Nor should we internalize the judgments of haters by questioning if there is something in us that justifies these responses and behaviors. Victims do not encourage violence simply because they choose to live their lives by their own cultural and social norms or because their modes of expression may differ.

Hatred, when parsed down to its bare essence, is ignorance searching for legitimacy. No one makes us hate other than those engaging in hate. Hate is the base answer to questions that the hater is struggling to answer. If hatred is a learned behavior, is it reasonable to assume it can be unlearned? Open dialogue and conversations with friends, family, neighbors, and colleagues are opportunities aimed at addressing the issues of prejudice and fostering inclusivity. No one race or culture has a monopoly on all that is good in man.

In the realm of poetry, emotions and ideas often find their most vivid expression through the power of words. The first poem delves deep into the darkest corners of human emotion—hatred. Through this poem, we are confronted with the chilling realities of hatred, a force that has shaped history, destroyed lives, and left scars on the collective soul of humanity.

The second poem offers a glimmer of hope and light in the face of such darkness. It celebrates unity, a force capable of healing wounds, bridging divides, and bringing people together. This poem serves as a reminder of the enduring human spirit that seeks connection, compassion, and harmony. I invite you on a journey through two distinct and profound verses, each a reflection of the human experience but on opposite ends of the emotional spectrum.

The Poems

Hatred Defeated

Within heated minds
Hatred's grip seeks to defeat,
Love's light breaks the storm.

Bound by shadows' grip,
Let virtue spring from within,
Hatred yields to love.

Deep-rooted darkness,
Minds entwined in bitter webs,
Love's light breaks the chains.

In shadows of spite,
Yearning minds seek the light's grace,
Compassion blooms strong.

Awash in venomous spite,
Mankind seeks higher purpose,
Love heals hearts' divide.

In shadows it dwells,
Hatred's grip tight and
unyielding,
Seeking light's embrace.

Through pages of thought,
Dissolve the poison's tendrils,
Reason's balm unfolds.

A symphony of minds,
Resonating empathy,
Healing rifts profound.

In wisdom's caress,
Harmony finds its triumph,
Hatred's fire subdued.

A Beacon of Hope

Amidst the chaos and the endless strife,
A call for unity breaks through the night,
A beacon of hope to guide our life.

In unity's embrace, we find the light,
A tapestry woven from threads so bright,
Amidst the chaos and the endless strife.

Diverse voices harmonize, taking flight,
Together we stand, strong and upright,
A beacon of hope to guide our life.

Through trials and storms, we hold each other tight,
Bound by a bond that feels so right,
Amidst the chaos and the endless strife.

Hand in hand, we reach for greater height,
Breaking down walls, tearing down the fight,
A beacon of hope to guide our life.

Let unity prevail, darkness takes its flight,
Together shape a world truly right,
Amidst the chaos and the endless strife,
A beacon of hope to guide our life.

Dear Reader, now it is your turn to write! Use this space below. Do not censor yourself.

Is hatred ignorance seeking legitimacy? How so?

Jacqueline Solimini, MPH, CPRC, is a holistic Complementary Health Practitioner, Certified Recovery Coach, Wellness Counselor, and Whole Food Plant-Based Nutritionist. Her work is centered on resilience training to help people build health-sustaining lifestyles minus chemical addictions and excuses. She specializes in helping clients overcome life's problems contributing to illness, daily anxiety, depression, and weight issues. Jackie graduated from Southern Connecticut State University, Albertus Magnus College, Cornell University, and Middlesex Community College. She is a two-time Amazon best-selling author. In 2020, Jackie founded Superformance Wellness Counseling, a remote/hybrid health and wellness counseling platform for individuals and organizations.

Contact: https://www.superformance.online

Chapter 25

When Poetry Ignites Your Soul

SkyyFlower

My Story

Poetry and I have a different love story. It's unique and embedded in healing and wellness. I've heard of the great poets and followed curriculum at school. But my soul was ignited when I discovered the poetry open mic.

As a child, my favorite class was creative writing. My teacher was a red-haired beauty with positive energy. I remember being most happy in that class—we wrote stories. I used my imagination and created using words. It seems during childhood I was free, until I wasn't. Between fifth grade and adulthood, many things occurred. I always journaled and wrote poetry, not realizing it helped me. I could think clearer and release things I didn't even know how to release. Fast forward to adulthood and therapy. I remember my therapist saying, "I think group therapy would be good for you. I think you should try it."

It was then that I realized the poetry open mic was my group therapy. I had been going for years and did my first poem at a hip-hop open mic. I felt incomplete. I had no idea about the poetry scene or poetry events. I knew no poets. When I discovered Busboys and Poets 14th and V and Pure Poetry First Wednesday at Pure Lounge on U St, I was sparked. I've been going ever since. June 2023 was Pure Poetry Live's 11th year anniversary!

I'm so grateful to Orville the Poet for igniting my soul through poetry. He created an event that changed my life. I was introduced to so many of the greatest poets on the planet by being in attendance at events every month, including Pure Poetry, Poet Life, Write like a Woman, Busboys and Poets weekly open mics at different locations, Brave Healer Productions, DMV RENAISSANCE AWARDS, and so much more. I then created my very own event company named Ignite the Soul Events.

When a poet delivers their poems at the open mic, it's exhilarating. Some are novices. Some are seasoned and well-practiced. Poets feel into what they share. Some are nervous and read from notes or books. Some give a show. The common denominator is they share from places within themselves. They give in hopes the hearer receives. They heal unknowingly and knowingly.

I healed unknowingly and later knowingly. I had to get into the energy and presence of powerful words. These words healed and helped me identify with my pain and joys, highs and lows, and laughter and tears. The subjects and topics range broadly across the mind: Love, relationships, politics, racism, economics, grief, loss of loved ones, tragedy, trauma, epiphanies, self-discovery, love of self, choosing life over depression.

I listened and observed and then began to sign the list at those open mic events. Those were "do it scared" moments. I was beyond nervous, but I was so welcomed, encouraged, loved, and supported. Everything I gave was reciprocated. Not to mention, most poets are entrepreneurs and business owners and/or have nonprofit organizations to help and support communities. I found my tribe.

I learned a lot about the structure of poetry events and found that some of my strengths included event management and executive concierge services. I want to take special care of the leadership of our industry—of the people taking care of the people. It's not easy creating a safe space for people to heal, especially when you're going through trials of life that wear you out. When your heart is big with wanting to help, you push through the tears, get out of bed, breathe, and practice. And you deliver healing messages while healing yourself and others.

Poetry ignited my soul in ways I'm eternally grateful for. I've healed in ways that enable me to continue my journey. I have so many memories of poets taking the stage, igniting my soul, and helping me move through my fears and anxiety.

The Poems

Gratitude to the Poets

pressing my way to poetry night, because the inspiration gives me life,
the energy
the positivity,
makes my wheels turn
to give as an intense yearn,
pouring out of the spirit.
Read it,
say it,
hear it.
I appreciate each and every poet, God's love,
they intellectually show it
as the words flow,
feeding your soul.
God's Spirit connects,
I know it.
Thank you, thank you, thank you
to the gifted.
the desire of your heart is for those hearing will be lifted.
Be encouraged
for you are an encouragement, walk in your vision.
Planted seeds will grow
as they are meant
with roots of great strength.
Thank you.
Peace.

Flow

I have thoughts,
I see images.
I have a vision,
order,
flow,
stress. What is that?
Why do we condition the power in our minds, capabilities?
build an empire
lift,
leave no one behind.
When you get there,
what will you do?
Get stuck
or
flourish,
spread the vision
possible,
give
and watch the hand of the Almighty

flow

It's Now O'Clock

(Call and response piece)

What time is it
It's NOW O'CLOCK

It's NOW O'CLOCK y'all
Fighting back from up against a wall

Change is HERE
Yeah Man I RELEASED FEAR

Cause God told me so
Cause Goddess says ASE' it shall BE SO

What time is it
It's NOW O'CLOCK

What time is it
It's NOW O'CLOCK

Gotta go Gotta go
It's Heavy Energy FLOW

My time is now
Like literally RIGHT NOW

I CHOOSE ME
I CHOOSE ME
I Set MYSELF FREE

How could anyone have the power to CAGE ME?

I take that POWER BACK UNAPOLOGETICALLY!

I can ONLY CONTROL ME
Seriously? Honestly? Wait what you thought YOU controlled me?

Not sorry at all to shock or confuse you.
As My Light shines brightly I thought you knew.

Knew this day would come
Now watch me embarrass my FREEDOM.

Carry on as you have in the past. I wish you a change that will last.

As my head is held high
The fear is released I shall soar with wings of an Eagle in the sky.

Amen and Ase'
Peace peace peace

Haiku

LISTEN LIGHTWORKER
UNDERSTAND THIS, they DO NOT
THIS AINT NO light work

Sorry for your loss
Wandering in disbelief
Sorry you are lost

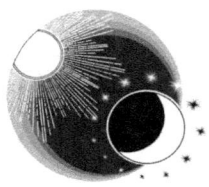

Dear reader, now it's your turn to write. Use the space below. Don't censor yourself.

Write a letter to Poetry expressing what poetry means to you.

Dear Poetry,

I Am SkyyFlower.

SKY
-represents I am limitless
Y
-find understanding
always ask questions
FLOWER
-represents the belief in peace, love, joy, prosperity, and wellness for ALL.

I am a poet on a wellness journey, building an empire, and walking in gratitude daily.

My given name is Kelly Marie Beech. I was born and raised in Washington DC. I spent summers in Kinston, North Carolina. I consider myself a city-country girl. I describe myself this way because I am a mix of high-energy innovation and southern hospitality. I believe in treating others the way I want my family to be treated. I also believe in building an empire based on unconditional love and solid foundations. Find Kelly on Facebook: @Kelly"SkyyFlower"Beech

Chapter 26

Soul Sessions: Poetry as Therapy

David D McLeod, DD, PhD, Certified Master Life Coach

My Story

"Hey, Diddle Diddle."

"London Bridge."

"Baa-Baa Black Sheep."

"Itsy-Bitsy Spider."

Like many children, I memorized nursery rhymes long before I could form complete sentences. Recollecting these titles, I instantly hear the faint echoes of my mom's soft voice as she sang to me and encouraged me to sing along; the memory brings with it a nostalgic wave of warm, loving tears.

My early experiences spawned a love of words and the infinite ways they can be arranged to create anything from the silliest ditties to the most awe-inspiring anthems, from the bawdiest quatrains to the boldest sonnets.

In school and university, I studied many great masters—Frost, Dickinson, Whitman, Shakespeare, and Browning, to name just a few. I learned all the rules, devoting myself to a full understanding of rhyme, rhythm, and meter, and I became adept at writing poems and songs.

But it wasn't until I encountered E.E. Cummings that I really began to see the magical power of poetry. Cummings had absorbed and transcended all the rules in favor of a new style that could hardly be called poetry in the traditional sense. Nevertheless, he and others like him paved a new way for people to express themselves. This unencumbered style fostered my discovery of an authentic voice to express my thoughts and find meaning in my life.

Serendipitously, in 1999, I was introduced to *Conversations with God* by Neale Donald Walsch, whose deeply spiritual subject matter set me on a profound path of growth I couldn't describe in ordinary words. I began journaling my spiritual experiences and delighted in watching my words emerge almost spontaneously in poetic form.

I have since come to view poetry and spirituality as close cousins—if not actual siblings. To me, all spirituality is poetic in nature (although the converse is not necessarily true). While ordinary prose is processed by the conscious mind, true poetry seems to bypass the mind to be processed in the soul. For this reason, poetry is like an unobstructed channel to the soul and is thus perfectly suited as a therapeutic mechanism for personal growth.

Over the years, I've composed many poems and songs, perhaps numbering into the thousands. Many have vanished into the dustbin of ancient memory, but quite a few persist in my life today.

As I was choosing pieces to share in this book, I found myself deeply immersed in the experience of the original events. I remember reading one poem and feeling deep compassion in my heart.

Wow! I marveled. *That actually happened! I was so insecure as a boy that I really did try to create an image of myself that I believed people would approve of. Thank God I found a way to reconnect to the truth of who I really am!*

Tears spilled down my cheek as I realized how much gratitude and joy has replaced all the resentment and misery of my youth. What a profound and healing gift that is!

I invite you to open yourself to a similar gift. No matter your age or your circumstances, journaling and poetry writing can serve you long into the future. Here is my suggestion:

- Read and digest poems of others.
- Find your voice and create poems of your own.
- Share your heart unabashedly with the world.
- Stand in the awesome truth of who you really are, with boundless love in your heart.

If you develop a practice as suggested here, you'll surely find a beautiful and unique path to your own healing.

The Poems

The Critic

The Critic wears a black cloak of derision over
    a designer tuxedo of humiliation.
A diamond stickpin of sharp sarcasm sparkles on his ascot,
        and of course there is a bright red rose of ardent shame
        pinned to his lapel.
His long golden locks are collected in a perfect ponytail
        of severe ridicule
        wrapped in a molded pewter clasp
        of judgment, belittlement and righteousness.
His hands are gloved in the pure white satin
        of perfectionism.
In one hand, he carries a black leather briefcase
        full of putdowns and epithets,
        and these he shares generously.
In the other hand is a cane
        made of highly polished acrimony,
        topped with a silver cobra's head full of contempt.
Most of the time his face is
        hidden in darkness
        but sometimes his teeth seem to leap into the light
        through a sneer of utter vilification.
He speaks often,
        but softly,
        in a voice of smooth hypnotic venom,
        and his quiet words mesmerize
        while slipping effortlessly
        into my heart.

When he first arrived,
  The Critic seemed simply a purveyor of information,
A guide,
Helping me to move toward perfection.
But as I became more invested in his ideas and ideals,
He seemed to exercise more power over me.
And as his power increased, so too did my fear.

Nowadays, the Critic follows me everywhere,
Like a shadow,
Keeping close watch over me,
                    (A stalker of fine proportion),
Ensuring that I am always aware of all my
            Weaknesses and foibles,
And reminding me that nothing I do is any good,
That I am not any good.

                              He seems to like his job.

I have tried many things to get him to leave,
But he says this is the way it is so I might as well accept it.
      I have tried threats.
      I have tried theatrics.
      I have tried begging.
      I have tried bribery.
Nothing has worked.
He just laughs and cajoles.

                              He seems to like his job.

            Tonight, something is different.

As I enter my sacred space,
My sacred place of creation,
I make a spontaneous decision to invite the Critic in.
He is taken aback.
He seems literally to retreat into the shadows.
I persist, saying
      "Please do come in.

I'd like to hear everything you have to say."
I prop the door open,
Step into the room,
And take my seat next to the computer.
    My heart is pounding so hard I can feel it on my tongue,
        But in a strange and contradictory way, I feel at peace.

After a while, the doorway darkens and the Critic steps in.
    "You are a pathetic loser."
His chest seems bigger than I remember it.
    "You think of yourself as creative,
    But you are only deluding yourself.
    Why don't you just give it up before
    You embarrass yourself completely?"
I say nothing, I just open myself to his words.
    "How can you possibly consider yourself a writer,
    With such drivel passing from your pen?
    A writer, indeed!
    A Hemingway of hogwash, that's what you are!"
With each word, he tries to stab me, to keep me down.

        But something has changed,
          And I just smile.

He moves a little closer toward me,
And with each step
The light of the room climbs up his leg,
    Up his torso,
        And moves toward his head.
            Something about the light...

*   Am I only imagining it,*
*   Or does he seem to be getting*
*   Smaller?*

"Look around you, little man.
How many people do you see reading your poems?
How many people do you hear singing your songs?
Where are the publishers to bring your works to light?
Where are the royalties to prove your worth in this world?
What a joke."

Strangely, I am unperturbed.
He stops.
Perhaps he senses this shift too.
    "Come, sit for a moment."
The gentleness of my voice surprises me.

I hear a sigh of exasperation,
Then all I hear is breathing.
    His breath and my own,
    Perfectly synchronized,
    Ricocheting against the silence.
        (Or is it just my own breath I hear?)
He slowly leans down toward me,
    The light giving way to the sneer,
        Then the base of his nose,
            Then the bridge of his nose,
                Then the eyes...

In that instant,
        As the eyes come into the light,
I realize the truth,
I realize what I am really looking at,
And I am no longer afraid.

It is I who begins to laugh,
As the deeper meaning of the secret reveals itself to me,
As the truth about acceptance becomes clearer.
    The Critic seems to fade,
Like San Francisco fog evaporating into sunlight,
But I can tell that he hasn't really left.
No, he is still there, where he has always been.

But even so, I feel lighter.

I turn to my word processor.
Words leap from my fingertips onto the blank screen.

Yes, much lighter.

Carpe Diem?

You didn't seize the day.
You took no risks at all.
You stayed there in the warm comfort of your bed,
     Playing it safe
Imagining what might be, what might have been.

There you slept, reveling in dreams,
Letting your consciousness float
On a sea of
     Wishes and hopes,
Wondering why things were the way they were.

You didn't seize the day.
You ceased seizing seasons of opportunity
     Long, long ago.
The bed was too inviting.

And where are you now?

Silk-lined walls
Materialized
When you weren't looking.

They embrace you in exquisite comfort
And keep you from falling
Into a world of pain.

No fear now!
Only total safety and security.
Nothing to harm you,
Nothing to fear.

Pay no attention
To the subtle creak of hinges
    As the lid slowly closes
    To hide all the paths
       You didn't take.

confession

   ladies and gentlemen,
    friends, colleagues, dear family,
and yes,
     you strangers in the back,

i stand here before you
    with cocoon unfurled
    clear, transparent, open
with all my scales and plates and filters piled here,
    still hot,
next to the base of the podium

i cannot say what power has brought me here
    today,
      at this time,
      at this moment

shame?
cowardice?
courage?

for me it is just a sublime moment

of long overdue awareness

i see the scars on your chests
i see the stripes on your backs
i see the welts
and bruises
and scrapes
and cuts
on your arms and legs

i see the shadows of grief and anguish
in the folds and creases and wrinkles
that you wear like necklaces and sashes
i see all these things and more
and i feel a fevered tugging at my heart
where even deeper hurt resides

because i recognize my signature
on so much of your pain

ladies and gentlemen,
i was crooked of heart
and twisted of mind
and my bent perspective sculpted this suffering

i dimmed your light in order to appear brighter
i trampled your presence in order to feel bigger
i lashed out and minimized you in order to magnify myself

i did these things because i was afraid

i was afraid to embrace compassion and love
because of a deeper fear
that to do so was a sign of weakness

i wanted to appear strong
but i ended up appearing weak
in spite of myself

so i confess my transgression
to each of you,

ladies and gentlemen,
friends, colleagues, dear family,
and yes,
        you strangers in the back,

i cannot say what power has brought me here
    today,
            at this time,
            at this moment

            but i am grateful for this space
    in which gentle truths
    throw back their heads
    and laugh
            with the pure joy of their liberation

legacy

i want to be remembered
    for my awareness of who i am
    for the expressiveness of my soul
    for the aliveness of my deepest essence

i want to be remembered
    for visions and dreams
    for generous sharings of deepest truth
    for loving without excuse or limitation

i want to be remembered
    for lofty floating thoughts that pass through me—
        smooth as blood
        coarse as muslin
        brief as a light-flicker—
    that cling to nothing
    and care not at all

(and never crack under pressure)

let no Authoritarian
     decide things on my behalf
let no Authoritarian
     presume to know me
let no Authoritarian
     control my fate
let no Authoritarian

(indulge the strange "fauxthority" elixir
running through its veins
and try to)

control anything!

in every town
   from equator
   to subtundra
people will have rejoiced
(and been rejoiced)
for the way they have lived life—
    not quietly,
    not subserviently,
    but brashly and unabashedly,
   without regret

people will be remembered
   by those who have chosen not to remember
     themselves
   by those who wish they had chosen
    differently
       i am among them
      and i want to remember it all

i want to remember it all
and i want to be remembered for all

this is the key to my
everythingness

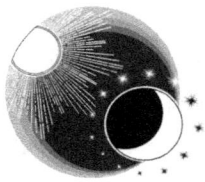

Dear Reader, It's your time to write! Use the blank space. Don't censor yourself.

As you contemplate my poems, you may find yourself resonating with some of my writing. Take a few minutes to reflect by considering how you deal with your inner critic, how you bring compassion and forgiveness into your life, and how you want to be remembered for all of the ways you show up.

Remember, healing is an ongoing process for everyone—a pathway to wholeness if you like. Find your voice and speak the truth that is in your heart so that you may experience the joy and blessing of incredible healing.

Namaste!

Fighter pilot. Best-selling author. Software engineer. Mentor. Aerobics instructor. Poet. Janitor. Lifeguard. Musician. Radio host. Graphics designer. Father. Student. Teacher. Photographer. Ordained minister. Yogi.

These roles—past and present—add up to a *LOT* of life experience, which David McLeod brings to bear in his capacity as a transformational speaker, life-mastery coach, experiential facilitator, and writer/storyteller.

As a Certified Master Life Coach with a PhD in Metaphysical Sciences and a DD in Holistic Personal Coaching, David creates and shares powerful *Life Mastery Tools* that enable adult men and women to transcend triggers, challenges, and obstacles so that they can express and experience the fullness of who they really are and thereby manifest truly magnificent and fulfilling lives.

Find out more about David and his offerings at https://yourlifemasterycoach.com

Chapter 27

Awakening the Senses Through Grace and Community

Heidi MacAlpine, OTD, Educator

My Story

> "The present is the only time in which any duty can be done or any grace received."
>
> **~ C.S. Lewis**

I always thought I had a pretty good understanding of what grace meant. Being brought up in the church and attending Catholic school for nine years, I heard the word being used frequently to explain Christ's love for us. Although I did not feel grace nor any sense of kindness or forgiveness from the women in black habits when blurting out conversations and words, it did teach me how to give grace to others and later to myself. I wanted to feel that transformation that felt lighter, more radiant, and filled with endless energy like the expressions "Walking on air" and

"On cloud nine." It just felt better, and it allowed me to shine for others. According to Webster's dictionary, grace is defined as a favor; good will; kindness; and disposition to oblige another. The free, unmerited love and favor of God. There was not any kindness displayed or a "Get out of Jail Free" card handed to me to better understand God's love when I made a mistake, but somehow, I learned from those experiences and others how to show kindness and goodwill even when we don't feel we have it in us.

I experienced moments of grace from different communities and overcoming my own obstacles due to illness or family tragedies throughout my sixty-one years. I went from bedridden to functioning and performing everyday activities I loved, needed, and wanted to do (occupations). By exploring and being curious about ways to improve my health and feel joy, I discovered simple and effective complementary therapies and tools that increased my energy and restored my health and functioning in a more meaningful way. Through my healing journey, I've been able to share my knowledge, intuition, and skills with others in similar situations

The two that come to mind have stayed with me and have touched my heart forever with grace. One was in May of 1988, the day of my father's wake. I truly felt the grace of my school community at a time when I felt so numb and disconnected.My world stopped that day, and my support system remained in my space of healing. The other more recent situation was where I experienced loveliness and grace on a whole different level in the space of my newfound friend in a nursing home with progressive multiple sclerosis.

Giving grace to others through my life experiences and chosen profession strengthened my understanding of grace. This reminds me of a poem by Gaiway Kinnel, titled Saint Francis and the Sow, in which he mentions that "Everything flowers from within, of self-blessing, though sometimes it is necessary to reteach a thing its loveliness."

I've found simple ways to reteach my friends, family members, and clients how to remain grateful for the smallest of accomplishments when overcoming barriers. Example: less pain in your neck when reading or looking at pictures on the wall when bedridden with a debilitating illness and sleeping through the night.

I learned what kindness can accomplish in its simplest form and how freely sharing your gift(s) with another person without any expectations can help both individuals feel their loveliness and value in their current situation, creating meaning with a sense of community.

The Poems

The following poems are reminders of those times when I felt a sense of community and alignment with spirit while tasting the sweetness and loveliness of it all.

Simple Senses, Curiosity, and Relearning Loveliness

Connecting minds,
Sharing ideas and tools
Making a difference,
Listening to hopes, dreams, and needs.
Curiosity to learn more.
A slight turn of the head
For a better view
of people and events
As digitized photographic memories
Reminds me of my past gone by
A stronger scent fills the nasal cavity.
My mind devoid of thought
And my body feels like a pool of jello.
Easing my anxiety
A mood booster
With a burst of orange and lemongrass
Suddenly I feel lovely,
Somehow lighter and energized.
I feel tingling in my head.
The synapses are firing within my brain.
Communicating on the loveliness it has absorbed.
Tones vibrate from the rose-colored quartz crystal bowl.
It sings for me!

A pure tone in the key of C
It resonates with me.
As skillful hands relax my body even more.
Gliding with grace over my shoulders, arms, and hands
Lavender has now called my mind to attention.
Lost in a moment of loveliness and gratitude.
Sensing a moment of relief with ease
With warmth and love
History unfolding
Hands holding
Body glowing
Filling the room with inner light
So bright
Releasing the fear, loneliness, and tension
Grace
Lifting spirits
Stimulating minds
Elevating moods
Rekindling a faith once lost
Meaning and purpose revived
I am more than the disease!
You are more capable.
I see you.
I hear you.
I know your worth.
Despite your challenges
and barriers
You push me to be more curious.
With grace
and a willingness to see your loveliness.
One sense,
One Simple solution,
One momen
Eyes, ears, and body
aligned and resonating with loveliness.

A Sense of Community

To those voices and sounds
That is like a ribbon dancing around my heart.
They facilitate and motivate.
Without words
Simple gestures
A bouquet of flowers
A meal
That somehow grounds me
Allowing me to feel
Without expecting anything from me
Yes! *I am here listening and aware of your kindness.*
I hear myself saying this, but my mouth isn't moving.
It feels like an empty space.
And an endless sea of words.
It is stored for retrieval later, just in case.
If you have experienced a disconnect after a tragedy
Then you know what I mean.
You are not alone.
In your comfortable state
of numbness
The community has made attempts to connect.
With meaning and heart-centered care to reconnect.
When silently retreated
You had gently awoken.
my senses
To mend
The tiniest pieces
Of my broken and splintered white picket fence.
Momentarily,
Dropping my defenses
Somehow my pain has changed my perception.
It has been cloudy without clarity.
These simple gestures

A smile,
A hug,
Lending an ear,
A warm, healthy meal
Brings light and feeling.
I'm listening!
I hear you!
I feel you in my space.
You are softening my pain.
Aww! Life!
I miss the strength and brightness of your vibrancy.
You!
My community is filled with love and grace.
Bringing back the light and colors
among the shading and shadows of doubt and uncertainty.

Dear reader, now it's your turn to write. Use the space below. Don't censor yourself.

I am inviting you to explore and understand simple and effective ways to gain clarity and direction when you or a loved one is overcoming life's challenges. It can be in one simple, mindful, and creative moment. There are endless possibilities at your fingertips (literally!). Although it is easily accessible on the internet, it is important to explore and research what works with your needs and your body. Are you curious about any techniques? A few ideas mentioned in the poems were new scents, like orange and lavender essential oil, or different breathing techniques that may help relax or excite you to overcome a hurdle or barrier while attaining your goals with meaning and purpose. If you are feeling uncertain, you can visit my website and explore some of the tips on my page or go to one of my podcasts, W.E.L.L. Matters, where I listen to Debra Battistella and I discuss wellness practices that we've explored and utilized for ourselves and our clients to restore or maintain health after various diagnoses and challenges or Improving Quality of Life through Wellness Practice, to learn about the tools I used during my wellness journey after my cancer and autoimmune diagnosis.

Heidi MacAlpine, a holistic therapist, podcaster, and owner of W.E.L.L. Alignment and Align OT is devoted to guiding children, adolescents, and adults in transitioning from mental health issues, trauma, and sensory differences with creative and meaningful activities that awaken the senses with a renewed sense of curiosity, confidence, and connection. This provides opportunities to express yourselves while engaged in meaningful occupations such as friendship, student, parent, and leisure activities. Heidi has used writing and poetry to move more smoothly through life's transitions with more purpose and clarity. She explores the sensations behind the emotion to help her clients make subtle to big shifts in their minds and bodies through Sensory Alignment Therapy, where clients become mindfully creative and curious while exploring different therapeutic tools such as movement, art, writing, sound therapy, and the Safe and Sound Protocol for a greater shift in awareness, potential, and emotional and physical wellbeing.

LinkedIn: http://www.linkedin.com/in/heidi-m-47370929

Chapter 28

Whispers of Wisdom:
Secret Spells and Codes for Sovereign Survival

Nydia Laysa Stone, Somatic Healing Artist, Therapist, and Coach

My Story

POWER OF WORD - CREATION OF REALITY
THOUGHT TO FORM - WORD TO MATTER

"SHAMBHALA," she said, sending shivers down my spine!

This word anchored into my body, awakening an ancient remembrance and deep longing.

". . .on the edge of physical reality. . .enlightened society. . ."

Holding my breath, heart pounding, I leaned over to eavesdrop. ". . .based on respect, wisdom, dignity. . .joy and bliss. . ."

I immediately fell under the magical spell of Shambhala!

I was 11.

Words had long become my safety line, my protective medicine, my elixir of resilience and survival; shields against the unpredictable grounds of my dysfunctional family life, they nourished my spirit and offered a certain control.

Words I heard, read, or invented became my Talisman—mighty guardians of secret portals I created in between the spaces, gateways to escape into hidden realms, feel safe, and meet my guides and ancestors.

I carried them in my pockets, my undies, and sheltered them under my pillow. I wrote them on stones, carved them into wooden sticks, and buried them in the ashes of my fires.

I was 9.

The lady sat close to my fire in front of the cave.

"Can I see your hands?"

Tracing my palm, her eyes sank deeply into mine.

She gifted me the picture of a Goddess.

"I love tigers!" I said, delighted. "Why does this woman have so many arms?"

"She'll protect you, my daughter. I'll sing you her song."

Her mantra sounded strangely familiar, like the mysterious dragonsongs I downloaded, sang, and danced to. Today, it's called light language.

These Sacred Codes were a powerful healing tool and remain my source of strength, inspiration, and joy along my journey.

Like mantras in Sanskrit or Celtic incantations, the Shamanic codes I invoke to open ceremonies create palpable vibrational alterations, rekindling remembrance of our ancestral wisdom, systemic heritage, and creative potential:

IN THE BEGINNING WAS THE WORD

Poetic masters taught me about ethics, values, bravery, respect; inspired and guided me to find my own voice, courage, and dignity.

Embodying these concepts, I awakened fearlessness within.

Through my poetry and stories, my 11-year-old runaway rebelled and affirmed that I was no longer submitting to violence and abuse.

An enormous power shift occurred!

I stepped out of the victimizing shame,
became a survivor.

I reclaimed my dignity,
the territory of my personal sovereignty.

BIRTHING NEW EARTH CONSCIOUSNESS
MICRO TO MACRO COSMOS - LOVE OVER FEAR

Personal sovereignty is the concept of independent authority, freedom of choice, expression, and integrity of your body, mind & spirit, and releases us from the cycles of power.

Once we disengage from the control and hope to receive fulfillment and validation from the outside, we find a place of authentic and self-generated power.

We can find our own answers and truth, follow our inner compass, and ancient Knowing, liberate from victim-hood and expand our challenges into growth.

Being the author of our life and reality and ultimately responsible for our beliefs, thoughts, intentions, values, emotions, actions and circumstances puts us in the driver's seat!!

Oh wow! How does THIS feel?
Exciting! - but also a bit scary, doesn't it?

No one is coming to save us.
No politicians, angels, aliens, or other entities.
We are the ones we've been waiting for.

Fear perpetuates the power cycle and keeps us vulnerable and controllable. Let's consciously choose the frequency of love!

Love is the concept of the Munay Ki - empowering Passage Rites, based on Andean Shamanism.

Planting these energetic 'seeds' to inform your DNA for potential transformation is my invitation for your vision quest to define a new expression of your life's reality.

Your sovereignty,

Your Shambhala!

The Poems

"You were born with wings, with potential, and dreams.
You were born with greatness - you were born with wings.
You are not meant for crawling, so don't.
You have wings.
Learn to use them and fly."
~Rumi

Shambhala: Sovereign Symphony
Feathers & Freedom

Here
I was safe.
Wild and free.
I was Queen. The One in power.
My word was respected and heard.
My body was sacred and untouchable.

I crafted my amulet of word birds and dragon songs

words of intention and powerful magic
fluttering through my mind, my heart
moving around in my mouth like candy
melting into me like dark chocolat
filling me with their sweetness and heaviness and lightness
so I felt nourished like after a big bowl of chocolat pudding, still warm,
sinking slowly, deeply
into my belly

soothing word creations, magical shields;
I could bite on them when I was in pain
and chew them up, when I was hungry for understanding and being seen
and loved.

Some tasted like warm honey, others like broken crystals,
or spicy, bitter, sour,
fiery red and scary black, dreamy golden and green and turquoise blue;

they lived in boxes, in the shells of snails, in trees, in nests, in
the dragon clouds,
under my pillow, in my back pockets and my undies - and they could fly away
with me
Words like birds
or dragons,
red balloons or dry leafs in the storm.

Some felt like the purging of my soul, of my innermost and vulnerable self,
liberating my essence
some were poisonous, full of rage
that found no other way of expression
than these bird words in disguise

Purging these words was such a relief!
like a huge exhale, bringing tears of exhaustion into my eyes
my breath eased once they were out of me

Some would smile at me and continue their journey
others would stay with me forever. We became best friends for life.
I could count on them being there when I called out in need of their
magic spells

Their rhythm picked up the beat of my heart and the longing of my soul,
made me dance and dream, drown and rise, sigh and sing and laugh

Sometimes there was just one, slowly emerging,
teasing my tongue, charming my mind
As it got born and danced up high
up into the starry skies - drawing shadows on the moons
free, ready to play with the mocking winds
under their wings
there was another one! growing,
I could feel it, taste it, smell it

word dancers, dragon dancers in the clouds,
hand in hand, one step, one word at a time
one wordbird after the other, breaking loose
from my mind, my mouth, my hands, my heart, and soul
to fly
the sky
was full of them

circling, turning, twisting, dancing, rising, falling, spiraling
much like these flocks of birds in thousands, moving like one being

a symphony, ever evolving,
of chaotic perfection and harmony
all in their graceful sovereignty
single birds, single
words

Today I Walk in Beauty

SCARS TO SERENITY - PAIN TO POWER

You showered me with Roses and Razorblades

In your wicked laboratory, you were
running your experiments on me
measuring, observing
with your distant, detached mind of a scientist.

I could feel your excitement
about every scream escaping my soul
and the burns and scars you left on me.

My skin was getting worn and raw, ripping open
in my most delicate and vulnerable places

my womanhood, my sacred Feminine, my flower
my heart, my soul

Always taking notes, loving gentleness in measured doses
you played me on the puppet strings of my own needinesss
my woundings of a child
keeping me in the destructive cycles of your games
because I had once learned that this
is love.

But I disentangled from your surgeon's grip and calculated cruelty;
ancient powers stirred within my core, my womb -
Resiliance!

No longer the submissive marionette, I ceased to dance to your manipulations.

Becoming Unchained

Once a willing dancer in the wicked waltz of an abusive narcissist
I now remember how to weave my tapestry of sovereignty;
with flames of courage, dignity of heart, I recognize
that love is not synonymous with pain.

Thank you for shattering this part of me
which only could respond to these old scars
so I could shed my skin - and
the skins of all my sisters, mothers, grandmother's - my entire lineage!
Ancient Ones! Thank you for the Blessing!

I stripped naked, layer by layer
invited my demons right into my life -
so they can't come and trigger me
out of the Blue

You watched the Phoenix Rising - and tried so hard to punish me!
but I did find the key!
I learned to loosen your grib and chains with the forces of Forgiveness
and set myself free.

Today
the power is mine

I smile at you and your attempts
your words have lost their razor cutting edges
they have no power over me
because today, I write my own words on my destiny

Today
I smile at you and walk away
a teasing swing in my hip
a smile glistening in my eye
joy in my heart
a song in my soul

Today
I walk in beauty
and the power is mine

Dear reader, now it's your turn to write! Use the space below. Don't censor yourself.

SOVEREIGNTY: Supreme power of independent authority, freedom of choice, and entire responsibility for our beliefs, emotions, circumstances, actions, and consequences.

If you claimed your personal sovereignty today with the snap of your fingers by choosing your magic words, spells, and codes:

What would you shed?
What would you call in?
What would change, and why?

Snap your fingers and get in the driver's seat!

Nydia Laysa Stone, somatic healing artist, socio-therapist, holistic healer and coach, is an experienced master teacher of the Healing Arts, Violet Flame and Divine energy attunements, Yoga, Dynamic Meditations, dance and art expression, sacred and shamanic ceremonies, and the Rites of the Munay Ki.

Nydia's passion is the alchemy of transformation, based on Tantric embodiment practices, somatic movement, vision quests, and passage rites.

Combined with the latest knowledge of neuroscience and therapy, these practices will bring you into remembrance of your ancient inner wisdom centers and systemic heritage to live the joyful, heart-centered life of your dreams and visions.

Nydia lives as a global nomad, mostly between the Caribbean, Crete, India, Bali, and Fiji Islands, and offers her signature retreat series worldwide, is engaged in and has created several charity projects. She loves animals and mangoes.

To work with Nydia, find her on social media or https://www.healingartsbynydia.com/

Chapter 29

The Everything That No One Sees

Ian Morris

My Story

William S. Burroughs, a luminary in the Beat Generation, revolutionized the world of literature with an unconventional writing technique: the cut-up method. This method, which involves dissecting and reassembling text to create new narratives, has become one of the most innovative literary tools of the 20th century. Born in 1914, Burroughs was introduced to the cut-up method by his friend Brion Gysin. Originally a technique used in visual arts, Burroughs adapted it into his writing process, creating a ripple effect in the literary world. He described the cut-up method as "a way of seeing." It's a tool to tap into the subconscious mind and bring forth ideas that might have otherwise remained hidden.

As a writer and blogger, I've found the cut-up method to be a powerful tool for innovation and creativity. It has allowed me to break free from conventional narrative structures and explore the boundless landscapes of my imagination. For instance, when faced with writer's block, I've utilized this method to dissect my existing content, rearrange it, and create something entirely new. It was like giving a second life to my words. But the benefits of the cut-up method extend beyond its creative potential. It has also served as a tool for personal healing. By deconstructing and reconstructing narratives, I've been able to reframe my perspective and rewrite my own story. It has given me a sense of control over my narrative, helping me confront and process my emotions in a therapeutic way. This personal experience reflects a broader concept: the power of creativity as a tool for healing. Humans are inherently expressive beings, and creativity is one of our most potent forms of self-expression.

Whether it's through writing, painting, music, or dance, creative outlets can serve as therapeutic tools to navigate life's complexities. Art therapy research supports this idea, suggesting that engaging in creative activities can reduce stress, improve self-esteem, and promote psychological healing. When we express ourselves creatively, we delve into our subconscious, exploring our thoughts, emotions, and experiences. This process can lead to self-discovery, personal growth, and healing.

In essence, William S. Burroughs' cut-up method is more than a literary technique. It's a testament to the power of creativity and its potential for healing. As writers and creators, we can embrace this method not only to innovate but also to navigate our personal journeys toward self-discovery and healing.

The Poems

An Experiment
in the Transfer of Energy

How can I write another love poem?

For that matter
how could any poet
ever write anything original
on the subject of love ever again?

It's all been said before

The act of love itself
is older than this rock
on which we sit
The whole process is just
an experiment in the transfer of energy is it not?

I say the answer
we are all searching for
lies in the structure
and the presentation of the page

Either you get them with the opening line
or you kill them with
the perfect grouping

of one-liners in closing
Either way it's always about the one-liners

'cause out there
they just want something they can recite to their lovers

Something that's easy to remember and helps make their struggle
a little less painful

For this
you will be a hero

but if you are one of the greats

I mean truly
one of the greats

then you have to come at it heart to page

where the gods decide
to pour through you and of you

Then you might have the pleasure and experience of co-creating
one of those poems

that shines from start to finish

Then your words will be revered for many years after your death

and maybe the schools will help kids dissect, letter by letter
each word you chose

Maybe they will even perform an autopsy on the meaning

If you're lucky

And maybe one day
they will all get it right

The meaning,
that is

The Everything That No One Sees

If love were a marketplace
then everything I found here in you would be for sale

Not front and center
or in the shop's window items

What we have here
is much deeper
and comes from years of searching

We lie on the road less traveled
we come from the hacking away at the overgrown and we will die
far off from
the beaten path

I've been turning through
these discarded hearts
and all these endless, winding roads

Searching for you this whole time

Only I didn't know it

It's the everything that no one sees that gave you away

Once that heart-glow of yours was pulled out
from its hiding place

every vagrant and thief for miles around stopped in their tracks

and are now en route to our position

I feel it's best
that we end this poem

and softly rest the back cover of this book against these rambunctious
words

A stern ending
but with the gentleness
of a kiss and a bed-time story

I will come for you
in my dreams tonight
and from here on out

God is With You

My meditation for today
shall be for me to simply go deeper
much like my poems
I just start with an idea that I want to focus on and then God whisks
me off light years away from this spot in which I sit

You can see how you would
feel the urge to share this type of experience with everyone

Yet the other day a friend of mine
told me a story of how people made fun of him for all the things he
said about God

The points he felt led to bring attention to
were about how we had all lost it and needed to be better people

and though in most cases I would agree with him this very moment,
here today, is different

Because with this type of approach how can they do anything else?

How can people who have never walked with fire and sat up for
weeks at a time

consumed with the spine tingles
and the feelings that come from

this type of interaction?

How can they
ever have any idea what God means to you

without ever knowing how deep the spring truly goes

Without hearing that voice calling
or the infinitely tall horns
that echo the sounds of love and compassion within

How can any of us here really claim to know anything

without walking with all of these fundamental building blocks of life

I say it all starts right here today
I say we should all work on getting to know one another better

Before our criticism is offered up
Before our individual judgments are served cold
Before we can even begin to understand each others' homeland
thought process

A loving agreement must be reached A friendship must be
constructed

Before any thoughts of monumental change can come to fruition

because I can tell you this from experience

God places with us a team
that is meant to progress us forward

This means the negative and the positive

This means we will call each other up in the middle of the night to
laugh
to cry
to talk about the burdens

to seek out a support system
so that we may return to the game tomorrow to the very same
position
with these very same scenarios

We are to do this
with the exact amount of love and feeling
that went into the attempts of yesterday
even if it sent us packing and running for the hills

I just mean to say that God is with you and will be forever
so let's work on each other

with a tenderness unseen before with more understanding

with more compassion
Let's work on our conversations with each other

so that we mend and heal rather than tear souls apart

This is my prayer
here today
That we may all fall in love more deeply

The Siege of Your Heart

Tonight I have come for you
That part of you that sleeps so deeply
That part that hides inside
those thick and fortified walls you've constructed

As your tower guards
are still sizing me up
searching for my intentions
I pace slowly the parameter
of your elaborate defenses

Crowds with opinions now gather

I hear their chatter growing stronger
which, in turn, gives your generals and soldiers

the courage to stand bold

They shout obscenities
and laugh so hard
they find it amazing
that a man
with no armor,

with no sword
or shield

would have the audacity to even dream of such

But I sing

I sing a song that drives your heart mad
and on each passing of the city gates
you hear its melody

Even now you feel it

vibrating and changing rhythms
You feel it fluttering like a captured firefly
bouncing off the sides of its glass jar prison

Just as he longs to be
set free
to those wide open spaces

So too, does your heart

She wants to run wild

with no fences or great walls of containment

Here we find ourselves
in a predicament that rivals the greatest of stories
and though you are the queen

here in this world
I will tell you every secret about yourself
in just a whisper

A whisper with the softness of a dim flickering candle warm and soothing
gentle and silent

If done correctly

a kiss could ward off
a thousand battles

and even better yet
if you apply the tactics of romance in such the right way

the enemy will never get the chance
to even draw their swords

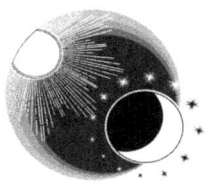

Dear reader, now it's your turn to write. Use the space below. Don't censor yourself.

Begin by selecting 12 random words from books or objects around you. Once you've got your words, it's time to weave them into a piece of poetic artistry. This could be a haiku, a sonnet, or even a free verse poem. Your next challenge is to use these words to craft an engaging title for your poem. You don't need to use all 12 words in the title; they are there to prompt and inspire your creativity.

This is not just a writing exercise but also an opportunity for growth and learning as a poet. So, take a deep breath, let your creativity flow, and enjoy the process!

Ian Morris is the founder of Listening to Smile, The creator of the LTS Method and Frequency Minded Music™. He is a renowned healer who has developed a unique approach to promoting wellness and self-discovery. The foundation of his methodology lies in Frequency Minded Music™ and The LTS Method, which combines healing frequencies and sounds to create a relaxing and stress-reducing experience Ian's holistic approach to healing is widely recognized as innovative and inspiring in the field of Sound Healing and frequency wellness. His work has touched countless people around the world, helping them discover their own unique path towards health and happiness. Listening to Smile is currently working in nine different countries with this groundbreaking work of Frequency Minded Music™

https://listeningtosmile.com

Chapter 30

Healing in the Pen: Writing for Wellness

Dawne 'Essence' Horizons, LMT, HHC

My Story

It was a day I will never forget! As I was walking through the lobby of the University Hospital back to my office as an administrative assistant, I began to see people in a different way, as if I had X-ray vision into their body and soul. It seemed as though everything slowed down; even time was going in slow motion.

I saw a woman walking towards me. I felt her pain so intensely, I could barely breathe. I said, "God, make it stop!" I took a breath and asked God what He wanted me to do.

He replied, "You have the answer."

I asked, "who me?"

He said, "Tell them."

And in the next few moments, my mind began to race, and God told me He was taking me on a journey, and that he'd use me to help others heal.

A few years later, pregnant for the fifth time, and going through a horrible divorce due to adultery, I heard God say, "Make healthy disciples."

Through my tears, hurt, and pain I agreed to submit myself to however God wanted to use me. I sat at the computer, and I prayed, "God please don't let me have a miserable baby." Well, He heard that prayer and she was a beautiful bright-eyed happy baby who brought joy and love to my heart. That baby attended holistic health certification classes with me. In fact, she went everywhere with me as I was strictly a breastfeeding mother. Today, that baby is 18 years old, working, driving, and still a joy (and pain) to me and the family.

And today, I'm the owner and operator of Dawne Horizons Spa & Wellness Center for the past 17 years! So, whatever you may be facing in life or in health and whatever you may have done, know that there is a God in heaven, and He loves you no matter what! All you have to do is believe and ask Him to help you. There were certainly many times when I didn't know how I was gonna make it, but one thing I knew for sure was with God anything was possible.

Everything I have ever been through, being born to a teenage mom, partially raised by my grandparents, attempted abduction, attempted rape multiple times, college, being stalked, getting born again and spirit filled, an abusive marriage, five children, a long tumultuous divorce, a custody battle, relocation to a new state, starting life and business again, struggling, becoming a caregiver for my mom with early onset dementia, grandchildren, my mom passing, and then losing everything I worked hard for in a few short months (my income, my house and almost my car and my health) has more than prepared me to educate, enlighten, inspire, and empower others to move from ruin to radiance in their lives.

Whether my hands on touch as a massage therapist, my inspirational word as an author and poet, or my words of wisdom as a keynote speaker, I am the epitome of possibility come to fruition. I'm able to help you transform your trauma to triumph and help you heal from the inside out. Great possibilities await you! Don't quit!

The Poem

Head Space

I'm in a space I've never been in before. Each day is a challenge. I mean I've certainly had challenging times before. I've traveled down many a rocky and rough roads. I've even climbed a few hills, dodged a few holes and trudged up a couple mountains. Haven't made it to the top yet but they say enjoy the journey, enjoy the climb. (Go figure!) Back to this space. My head space. It's uncomfortable, however not confining. It's challenging but not defeating. I think. I hope. I pray. Ugh!

I've been through some tough times, but this space is different. It's hard to explain really. For someone who writes and often has a way with words I'm almost speechless. I mean I have words just not sure they'll make sense. I'm trying to make dollars but this head space keeps changing my thoughts, and it makes no sense, it's hard to focus, even my distractions have distractions.

I know I'll get through it even though I don't yet see the light at the end of the tunnel. Trust me, I know this too shall pass and that's what I tell myself, this too shall pass. I'll pass through to the end of the tunnel, eventually. It's not dark and I'm glad for that, but it sure is cloudy. Probably just smoke and mirrors but I can't seem to clean them. I mean get free of this strange mentality. This feeling of not being myself or my 'normal' self. Of knowing what to say and what to think but not being able to hold the right thoughts. Being barraged by thoughts and distractions.

It's frustrating and stressful but I know the way out. You see I dig myself out every day and have a good day the next day but the day after that, I'm back in the thoughts and feeling uncomfortable, stressed, overwhelmed, frustrated with these complicated thoughts then trying to weave my way out of this madness so I don't become a basket case or a statistic. All my normal pick me ups are not lifting me up high enough to get picked up, above this stuff but yet just enough to get through to another day.

I don't know why I'm feeling this way. Well at least I'm feeling, even though I can't cry. I'm not sure why and then sometimes out of the clear blue sky and at the most in opportune times, like being on the phone with customer service trying to fix my subscription and the wells begin to fill up and I just wanna break the dam, but I can't lose my water while on the phone that would be out of order, so I stuff it back inside until I'm done but then it's done and no longer ready to fall or even leak out. I feel like I'm walking around all day with a pout. So much in my head but I can't let it out.

I'm the strong one, all is resting on me, all is looking to me, why can't I just be weak for a day, for a moment. Wait, maybe that's what's happening. Maybe that's the space I've been flowing in and out of. Weak a day, strong a day. Up a day, down a day. High a day, low a day. This is not, however, what I meant when I said be weak for a moment. I meant weak to let it out and not having to be so strong and hold it in. What I really meant was a break. Yeah, a much needed break from chores and responsibilities and people looking to me to make ways out of no ways and stretch the food and the money, provide the needs and the wants, but all I want, is to feel loved and appreciated. I want to be seen and heard.

All I want is to be cared for, like I care for others. All I want is to be wanted, for me, the real me and not what I can give. All I want is to let go, without being let down. All I want is a break, a breath, a pause for the cause, of my mental health, of my emotional health, of my physical health and I won't even open that Pandora's box for now, I'll keep it locked. But, I do need to breathe. I need to move into a new head space. An open space. A loving space. A free space. A clear space, is that even a real place? Help me Lord deliver me from this place where my head space, is in space and I just wanna get back home to my rightful place.

Dear reader, now it's your turn to write! Use the space below. Don't censor yourself.

I feel the most free when I _____.

Essence: The poet, massage therapist, holistic health coach, empowerment speaker, and author, also known as Dawne Horizons, has been writing since the age of nine. She's an inspirational, empowering poet bringing healing to your mind, body, and soul. Essence helps others to recognize their greatness and pursue their purpose with passion. She has performed all over the DC Metro Area. You can find her poetry book entitled, *Spoken Words from the Heart: Life, Love & Intimacy* available now on her website and Amazon. Essence is a mother of five adult children and grandmother of four.

If my story or poem resonated with you or you want help to clear your mind and begin again, then connect with me to get your free, Writing for Wellness eBook and be sure to follow me on all social media @dawnehorizons. You can also join my free Facebook group: Wellness Wisdom for Women.

https://www.askdawne.com/

Chapter 31

The End is the Beginning of Everything Good

Laura Di Franco

When you get to the end of this book, it's really just the beginning because the question becomes: Now what?

Well, I have your answer, and it's good.

Go back through and find the poems and poets who struck a chord, gave you goosebumps, or otherwise sparked possibility inside you. Maybe your perspective shifted, or you realized an opportunity. These amazing souls are waiting for you to reach out to them. Send them a note and let them know what you thought about their poems. Tell them what you loved. Share your ahas.

Each one of my author-poets has so many more gifts to share through their writing or businesses. They've devoted their lives to helping people like you thrive. Be brave and click on their website links, find them on social media, and reach out with a note.

Maybe you have a dream that you haven't put into action yet. Maybe you're feeling stuck and don't know which way to go. The authors in this book aren't just poets; they're master healers, coaches, therapists, artists, and professionals who can be the next step on your journey.

What if there's someone you haven't met yet, or something you haven't learned yet that could change everything?

We want this book to be a starting point for everything good to come!

Before I get to the thank you page, I'll leave you with one of the very first poems I wrote after meeting Jude that fateful day when I claimed the title of poet. Enjoy!

The Stars Are Enough

Some small sound shakes me from sleep
A call from inside a dream.
Silver-blue light draws me out
beaming a window-shaped box on the floor.
Ah the moon, of course, calling my name.
Taking my bare feet outside
the warm silent breeze floats around my skin
and I lift my eyes to the sky.
If I ever wondered about miracles and life
or purpose and God, or love,
the trillion tiny sparkles of diamond light
making maps for ships
and falling for wishes
would have me believe.
The stars are enough.

MORE ABOUT LEAD AUTHOR,
POET, AND PUBLISHER LAURA DI FRANCO

I was born in San Francisco, California, grew up in Marin County, and went to San Francisco State University, where I played two years of soccer. I moved to the East Coast right after physical therapy school to be with my boyfriend (now ex-husband). I was the first in my family to ever live anywhere else but California until recently, when my sister and mom both moved close to the area I'm living in now, which is Bethesda, Maryland.

I spent the first half of my life as a severe introvert, extremely shy, and unable to feel worthy enough to stand on a stage, let alone be the reason others stood on one. Being an athlete saved me during the first half of my life. That's where I belonged and excelled. I was a soccer player, marathon runner, and black belt in Taekwondo, and have been a lifelong lover of figuring out what my body-mind is capable of. That served me well when I became a holistic physical therapist and started helping others heal.

I can say with confidence that every single event in my life served me well. I don't have any regrets or wishes to do things over.

I'm happy to say things have changed in the "shy" and "introvert" departments. While I'm still a traditional introvert (I recharge with alone time), I happily call myself an extroverted introvert these days. My last decade was more about finding out what I'm capable of in the mind-soul areas. This pursuit changed everything for me. I've mastered my mindset, and that continues to create miracles.

Shifting from physical therapist and healer to publisher in 2020 was one of the scariest moments of my life—one of my identity crises but also miracles. Even though Brave Healer Productions was founded before that (2016), I didn't claim the title of "publisher" until more recently, and it took a huge leap of faith to let my physical therapist hat go. And it was the best thing I've ever done.

What, exactly, was the best thing I've ever done? Following my joy, passion, and soul and following the obvious breadcrumbs the Universe left me. I'm so glad I was brave enough to take the leap.

Because here I am, writing this note to you, in my first poetry book collaboration with a community of healer-poets who are changing the world together. It's amazing. I'm so grateful.

There's more "about me," but if you want to know more, I invite you to connect and schedule a chat. What I know for sure is that the incredible empire that is Brave Healer Productions was built on the spirit of connection. And I can't wait to connect with you!

Please find more poetry (written and spoken) in the following two places:

Warrior Love, the Facebook Poetry Page:
https://www.facebook.com/warriorlove/

On YouTube: Positively Purposeful Poetry:
https://www.youtube.com/@positivelypurposefulpoetry8316

For inquires about our next poetry book project, writers' retreat, writers' circle, course platform, or online and local events, find everything at BraveHealer.com

ACKNOWLEDGMENTS

My gratitude is shared today with a full heart and deep joy. Gratitude makes magic, creates abundance, and raises the vibe, and this poetry gratitude vibe is about as high as it gets!

To every poet who said yes and joined me on this journey, you light my fire in ways you may not understand. This is soul work. It's legacy work. And the fact you wanted to help me move these brave words and work into the world is proof that I'm living my purpose. Thank you from every corner and crevice of my being.

To the women in the dedication who stoked my poetry flame: Jude Christensen, Ginny Robertson, Laura Munson, and Dinahsta "Miss Kiane" Thomas—thank you for seeing me and my poetry.

To my open mic poetry family who've listened, heard, and seen me, shaking or not, thanks to every one of you for your snaps and claps. Special thanks to KaNikki Jakarta, the first-Monday hostess at Busboys and Poets in Virginia and author-publisher-poet-goddess extraordinaire. I love you, and I'm so grateful to know you. You helped me keep going.

To Tanya Stokes, our cover designer—thank you for bringing my moon-sun cover vision to life. I'm so grateful for your passion, talent, and the beauty you're helping me share with the world.

To Kelly Kaschula, Brave Healer Productions Publishing Manager and Brave Kids Books Director. Thank you for your brilliant design of this book interior! We're waking the world up to what's possible together. Thank you for seeing my vision and for helping to bring it to life.

To Maggie McLaughlin, our Amazon Pro. Thank you for helping every book title arrive into the world seamlessly and on schedule! You are a gift to us!

And to all poetry lovers everywhere—especially the book launch team who helped us get this book into the world in a bigger way—thank you for your passion, love, and support.

THE NEXT BRAVE HEALER PRODUCTIONS BOOK

We're working on our collaboration books for the upcoming year!

If you're a poet or writer in the holistic health and wellness field interested in collaborating in our next book, or you have ideas about leading your own book collaboration, we'd love to chat with you! Reach out to support@lauradifranco.com and let us know!

To see a list of book projects we're working on, go to: https://lauradifranco.com/expert-book-collaborations/

I Fly With Angels

Let's run away
stare at the moon
stay warm
under the covers
much too long

Let's spend the day
dreaming
make magic
love
and stardust

Let's taste bliss
on our lips
under a sky
glowing
with possibility

Keep me
held gently
in the soft space
of your sweet soul
and smile

Remind me
to feel
breathe
believe
and laugh

Let's run away
to a place
we can be
wild
with desire

Light me up
then
come linger
by my fire
a little longer

Remind me
to be urgent
about my joy
not waste a drop
not wait one moment

Run with me
and my crazy
toward the cliff
jump into my heart
don't look back

Trust me
I have wings
I have ecstasy
I fly
with angels

And you, my dear reader, fly with angels, too. My wish for you is that through every soul-filled word in this book, you feel the love, joy, and truth that is you—a spark of the divine.

Big warrior love,

Laura